COMPASSIONATE REVOLUTIONARIES

THE MORAVIAN ANCESTORS

OF

GEORGE W. BUSH

Fred J. Milligan

HERITAGE BOOKS, INC.

Published 2001 by

HERITAGE BOOKS, INC.
1540E Pointer Ridge Place
Bowie, Maryland 20716
1-800-398-7709
www.heritagebooks.com

ISBN 0-7884-1934-X

A Complete Catalog Listing Hundreds of Titles
On History, Genealogy, and Americana
Available Free Upon Request

To my wife Carol Moreland Milligan, fifth cousin of Barbara Bush, wife of President George H. W. Bush and mother of President George W. Bush. Both are 4th great granddaughters of Christoph and Susannah Klein Demuth, Moravian pioneers, who settled in Gnadenhutten, Ohio, in 1803, the year Ohio became a State.

But whoso hath this world's good, and seeth his brother have need, and shutteth up his bowels of compassion from him, how dwelleth the love of God in him? My little children, let us not love in word, neither in tongue; but in deed and in truth.

- I John, chapter 3, verse 17, King James Bible

TABLE OF CONTENTS

CHAPTER 1

COMPASSION IN A HOSTILE WORLD

The President's description of himself as a compassionate conservative has focused attention on the role of compassion in human affairs. Although great men have frequently praised the value of compassion, the tortured history of mankind demonstrates in graphic detail that its influence has been limited. This has been particularly true when people find themselves in hostile situations. When attacked or threatened, people react with anger, even hate, and sometimes violence. When under stress, the heart often grows cold. The natural well springs of compassion run dry. Some say this is human nature, as if to suggest that people have no choice but to react in this way. Others say it is common sense, because allowing compassion to influence a decision in a hostile situation is foolish. On the other hand, others believe that compassion represents the best in mankind and that people have the capacity to react with compassion even when surrounded by hostility. According to this view, if compassion had a greater influence on actions, the world would be a much better place.

The President's description of himself as compassionate has special meaning to Christians. Although compassion is highly valued by many who are not Christians, it is an important part of the Christian faith. Jesus told of a Good Samaritan who observed a traveler robbed by thieves and left naked and half dead upon the road. Jesus described the Samaritan's reaction, "When he observed him, he had compassion on him."[1] Unlike a priest and Levite who passed by on the other side of the road, the compassionate Samaritan bound up the injured traveler's wounds and took him to an Inn where he paid the Innkeeper to take care of him. Jesus taught that the second greatest commandment was, "Thou shalt love thy neighbor as thyself."[2] He taught that the duty to love extends even further than neighbors when he said, "Love your enemies, do good to them that hate you."[3] By describing himself as a compassionate conservative, the President reassured Christians that he recognized his Christian duty to be compassionate.

Despite the President's assurances, many would question to what extent a President can and should be compassionate. The nation has enemies who are constantly testing the President's ability and willingness to defend its interests. Powerful businesses, industries, labor unions, and trade and professional associations seek to advance their interests by competing for the President's favor. They frequently attack him if he disagrees with them. Politicians, political parties, groups interested in economic, environmental and social issues, and electronic and print media seeking to increase their ratings compete for the public's attention and their competition frequently arouses the emotion and rhetoric of war. The President exercises his responsiblities at the center of a hostile world of international relations, politics, business, and media glare. Striving to be compassionate in such a world must indeed be a formidable challenge.

---

[1] Luke, chapter 10, verse 33, *King James Bible*
[2] Matthew, chapter 22, verses 37-40, *King James Bible*
[3] Luke, chapter 6, verses 27 and 28, *King James Bible*

Although the challenge facing the President is awesome, it is not unique. Millions of people in America and throughout the world strive to live compassionate lives in a hostile world. They may face fierce competition in business or in their career. They may suffer from an abusive marriage partner or parent. They may live in a dangerous neighborhood or even a war zone. They can react to their situation with anger, hate, and even violence, or they can turn their suffering into compassion for the suffering of others.

History is the grand stadium where faith, hope and love compete against their old adversaries anger, hate, fear, avarice, and pride for the souls of mankind. The consequences of choices are frozen in time forever to be debated and judged worthy of emulation or condemned to the smoldering trash pile of human cruelty, greed and folly. With this in mind we turn to the story of the Moravian missionaries who came to these shores inflamed with Christian compassion only to see their hopes for bringing Christianity to the Indians dashed on the cold, hard rocks of of hate, anger and violence. The story is not about their failure. It is about their commitment, a story made more interesting by the fact that among those early missionaries were ancestors of George W. Bush, a President committed to discharging his awesome duties with compassion.

Some of the President's ancestors on his mother's side belonged to a little-known evangelical Christian Church whose members devoted their lives to Christ's teachings about compassion. This book tells the story of their commitment, a commitment that brought them suffering and even death. Despite repeated set backs, disappointments, and even defeats, they maintained their hope and commitment that compassion would triumph over hate. Because they challenged the accepted wisdom as to the possibilities for mankind, I have called them compassionate revolutionaries.

3

These ancestors were members of what today is called the Moravian Church. This Church is one of the oldest Protestant churches. Its early history in the ancient kingdoms of Bohemia and Moravia is a story of survival despite constant persecution. The persecution brought the Church nearly to extinction until some of the surviving faithful fled their homeland to a compassionate nobleman's estate in Saxony where they found sanctuary. The Church was reorganized there in 1727. Some of President Bush's ancestors were among those who abandoned their homes and possessions to participate in that reorganization and renewal. They were among the early missionaries sent by the Church to North America to bring Christianity to the Indians, arriving in Georgia in 1735 and 1736. In 1741 and 1742 they helped with the founding and construction of the Moravian community at Bethlehem, Pennsylvania, which became the Church's headquarters in the United States, and its base for missionary work. Their work helped support the Moravians' missions to the Indians in Pennsylvania. They were among the first Moravian settlers who moved to Ohio to support the mission to the Indians on the Muskingum.

The story covers the period when America grew from a few small British colonies along the eastern seaboard to the establishment of a new nation comprised of peoples from diverse cultures and its expansion across the Appalachians into the Ohio country. It shows how a peace-loving people who believed and sought to live by Christ's admonition to love one's enemies survived the war between England and Spain over Georgia, King George's War, the French and Indian War, Pontiac's War, Lord Dunmore's War, the Revolutionary War, the Indian Wars that opened up Ohio to settlement, and the War of 1812.

4

CHAPTER 2

ANCIENT UNITY OF THE BRETHREN

The Moravian Church began in the Kingdom of Bohemia and spread to neighboring Moravia. These ancient kingdoms are now part of the Czech Republic and Slovakia. The area is located east of Germany, north of Austria and Hungary, and south of Poland. The Church is one of the oldest Protestant churches in the world, and its origin sheds light on the character and practices of the Moravians who came to America.

The Moravian Church traces its origins to John Hus, a priest from Prague, who was burned at the stake for heresy on July 6, 1415. This was a time when there was but one official church in Western Europe, the Church of Rome. Hus incurred the wrath of the leaders of the Church of Rome by preaching that the Bible was a higher authority than the Pope, cardinals, bishops and priests. He criticized the corruption that was rampant in the church at that time, and attacked the church for raising money by selling indulgences that purported to grant forgiveness of sins to the purchaser. The Pope sent representatives with large chests full of the indulgences that were placed in all the major churches. People lined up to buy forgiveness for their sins. The chests were not allowed in the

Chapel of Bethlehem where Hus preached. To the people gathered in his Church, he defiantly preached that no Pope or bishop had the power to forgive sins. Only God through Christ had that power, and He only pardons the sincerely penitent.

How did this man of simple peasant background develop the courage to defy the Pope, the most powerful man in Europe? The death of his father at a young age left Hus in the care of his single mother. A pious Christian who recognized the value of education, she brought him up to love the Lord and encouraged his attendance and studies at a country school. Because of his great promise, he was admitted to the University of Prague as a charity student where he excelled. Hus not only learned the Bible, he based his life upon the teachings of Christ. Upon graduation he entered the priesthood. He also taught at the University of Prague and served as rector of the University, which was one of the foremost universities in Europe at the time. He became the priest at the Chapel of Bethlehem in Prague.

Hus was highly regarded in Prague. Although called a chapel, the building where he preached held over a thousand, and Hus drew large crowds. In the other churches, services were conducted in Latin, but Hus preached and wrote hymns in the Czech language. According to Hus, the Czech language was as precious to God as Latin. In his sermons he read to the people what the Bible said and then contrasted that with the actual practices and teachings of the Roman Church. In his sermons he drew heavily on the teachings of John Wycliffe, an Englishman, who lived from 1324 to 1384.

At first it may seem peculiar that a priest in Bohemia would be acquainted with the teachings of an Englishman from the other side of Europe. However, the queen of England was a Bohemian princess who embraced Wycliffe's teachings and encouraged their circulation in her native country. Jerome, a citizen of Prague, upon return from England brought Wycliffe's writings and shared them with Hus who read them with interest. Wycliffe had attacked the corruption of the church. He believed it had been corrupted by wealth and its involvement in political affairs. He taught that the Bible was a higher authority than the Pope. He urged the translation of the Bible into English and proposed the creation of a new order of "poor preachers" who would preach to the people from the English Bible. He said that they should model their lives after the apostles who spread out among the people following the death of Jesus. As a result of his efforts the Bible was translated into English and itinerant preachers, nicknamed Lollards, were sent out in pairs, barefoot, dressed in long monk's robes, each carrying a staff. They talked to people on the roads, on the village greens, in the fields, and in churchyards and taught them the Lord's Prayer, Ten Commandments, and other basic Christian teachings. Two followers of Wycliffe came to Prague and tried to spread his views. When they were forbidden, they drew two pictures on a wall. One was a picture of Jesus entering Jerusalem meek and sitting upon an ass followed by his disciples in travel worn garments and bare feet. The other was a picture of the Pope arrayed in rich robes and triple crown, mounted upon a horse magnificently adorned, preceded by trumpeters and followed by cardinals and prelates in dazzling array. Crowds came to gaze upon the two pictures and thought about the contrast between the meekness and humility of Jesus and the arrogance of the Pope who claimed to be his servant.

Although admired and protected by the King and Queen of Bohemia, Hus angered the Pope and his cardinals. Rome first tried to silence him by excommunicating him and placing Prague under interdiction. Interdiction meant that the churches were closed and sacraments such as marriage, baptism, and the last rites could not be performed. Needless to say, this created a furor among the people. In order to spare the residents of Prague further suffering, Hus left Prague and returned to his country village. He had not been silenced however, because he continued to preach in the countryside, and his writings were widely circulated. After the furor in Prague subsided, he returned to the Chapel at Bethlehem and preached with all his former courage and zeal.

The Roman Church was in trouble. Three men claimed to be Pope and competed for money, soldiers, and allegiance. They not only waged verbal wars against each other, but also threatened to involve their followers in military contests. Hus bravely protested against the terrible actions that were being taken in the name of religion. Many people began to blame the church leadership for the problems of Christian Europe. The church leaders believed the teachings of Wycliffe and Hus and their followers were threatening their spiritual authority and the legitimacy of their economic and political power. Rather than try to correct their own shortcomings, their strategy was to attack those who dared criticize them. The Emperor of the Holy Roman Empire called for a Council at Constance near Switzerland to heal the divisions in the church caused by the three contending popes and to root out heresy. The leaders of the church and kings or their representatives convened. The Pope and his challengers were summoned to appear. Hus also received a summons, and the Emperor and the King of Bohemia guaranteed his safety.

Notwithstanding the safe-conduct that he received from the Emperor and King, Hus had no illusions about what awaited him at Constance. He wrote to one of his friends that he knew he was going to face his mortal enemies, which could lead to suffering and even death. He trusted in God to give him the strength to speak truthfully and with wisdom no matter what the consequence. If Jesus, with all his innocence and power, was willing to suffer and die, then why should not he, a contemptible mortal, be willing to do the same for the glory of God, and the salvation of his soul. On his way to Constance people turned out to meet him, and magistrates escorted him through villages. It was like Jesus triumphant entrace to Jerusalem before His arrest and crucifixion.

Upon arrival at Constance, the Pope assured Hus that he would be protected. However, within a short time he was arrested and imprisoned in a loathsome dungeon by order of the Pope and cardinals. Powerful noblemen from Bohemia expressed outrage at the violation of the safe-conduct that he had been given. However, Hus's enemies convinced the Emperor that he need not keep a promise made to a heretic. The damp foul air of the dungeon nearly killed him, but he refused to retract his views. Weakened by months of imprisonment and illness, he was brought to trial before the Emperor in chains. He defiantly challenged his accusers to point to the passages of the Bible that proved his teachings were false. He courageously repeated his protest against corruption within the church. He was convicted of heresy and was required to choose between recanting his views or death. For Hus this was no choice. When he was returned to his cell, he knew this would be his last night on earth. The next day he was again brought before the Emperor and church leaders and once again asked if he would admit his errors. When he refused, his priest's robes were taken from him, a tall fools cap decorated with three devils fighting for his soul was placed on his head, and he was marched to the stake where he was given a final opportunity to escape death. He replied that he preferred to die with joy in the faith of the gospel which he had preached. The fire was ignited, and he began singing a hymn and continued singing until the fire extinguished his life. As a final humiliation, his ashes were gathered and thrown into the Rhine. The Council also condemned and burned Hus's friend Jerome at the stake. It even ordered that Wycliffe's bones, which had been buried for over thirty years, be dug up and thrown into a river. The Council did resolve the schism in the Church by appointing a new Pope, but it did nothing about the corruption in the Church.

As in living so in dying, Hus followed his Savior's example. Like Jesus he recognized that his death was necessary and faced it without fear. Jesus had criticized the high priests of Jerusalem and had chased the money changers from the Temple. Hus had criticized the church hierarchy and criticized the sale of indulgences in the church. The high priests had Jesus arrested and taken before the Roman governor to be executed. The Pope had Hus arrested and taken before the Emperor to be executed. In both cases the religious leaders felt threatened by someone who spoke truthfully from the heart. In each case the execution of the messenger immortalized the message and doomed the executioners to condemnation by the universal judgment of mankind.

After the crucifixion, Jesus' disciples did not seek revenge, plan a revolution or commit acts of terrorism. They taught love and forgiveness. Stephen, Peter and Paul were among those who suffered a martyr's death. Thousands more were to follow their example. Each time a Christian died for the faith, hundreds more were converted. Despite constant persecution, Christianity spread across the Roman Empire and finally in 313 AD Emperor Constantine granted religious toleration to Christians. When the Roman Empire fell, Christianity survived. Those who watched Jesus die on the cross could not possibly have imagined that his teaching about love, compassion, and forgiveness would spread throughout the Roman Empire and beyond among millions of people who previously had no knowledge of the Hebrew God. As they witnessed the power of the Roman Empire take the life of someone as innocent and harmless as Jesus seemed to be, how could they possibly have thought that his teachings would survive in the lives of millions of committed followers while the Roman Empire would become nothing more than old ruins and ancient stories of interest only to archaeologists and students of antiquities. His followers' only weapons were the power of the message and their commitment, which gave them the strength to overcome suffering and even death.

Christianity had triumphed, but what had it become? How by the time of Hus had the leaders of Christ's church come to act like the high priests who had Jesus crucified? In the year 800 the Bishop of Rome crowned Charlemagne, who was King of the Franks, as Emperor of the Holy Roman Empire and successor to the Emperors of the old Roman Empire. By so doing, he convinced the people that the worldly power, which they associated with the old Roman Emperors, and the power of God were united. Thus began a powerful alliance to create a powerful political structure based on the people's religious faith. No political structure will last long based on force alone. It must have legitimacy to keep people's voluntary allegiance and willingness to sacrifice. The Emperor offered military and legal protection for the church, and the church offered legitimacy to the Emperor and the threat of Hell for people who failed to obey him. As is so often the case, power led to corruption. In its beginning the Christian church was based on persuasion and the free choice and personal commitment of its members. By the time of Hus allegiance to the church was enforced by threats and coercion, and church leaders had come to act like political leaders with totalitarian power. Like Hitler and Stalin they would not tolerate anyone who questioned their authority. Any challenge to their authority was heresy, and heresy was punished by death.

The execution of Hus caused outrage and a revolt against the Roman Church in Bohemia. The Roman Church no longer had any legitimacy in the minds of most Bohemians, and Hus' courage in the face of death convinced them that the Church leaders in Rome had no power over people who were not afraid to die for what they believed. The Pope and the Emperor were to learn the power of people inspired by a martyr's death. The contest became a political revolt. The

Bohemians wanted no part of the Church of Rome or the Emperor who had done its bidding. They wanted to define their own national identity and control their own religious institutions.

The Hussites were denied the use of church buildings so they held services in open fields. A hill called Mt. Tabor became one of their rallying places. On July 22, 1419, forty thousand persons gathered there from all over the kingdom to share in a national communion service. Since Roman priests denied the people wine at communion, the communion cup became the symbol for Hussite unity.

In 1419 following a riot in Prague during which several members of the council were thrown to their death from a high window in the building housing the council chamber, the Emperor and Pope launched a crusade to crush the Hussites. John Ziska, a leader of the Hussites took command. Sixty-six years old and blind in one eye, he rallied the peasants and towns folk to defend their homes and their faith. He urged them to have constantly before their eyes the Divine Law and the common good, and invited anyone who knew how to handle a knife or throw a stone or brandish a cup to join the march! Ziska composed the Hussite battle hymn, "Ye Who the Lord God's Warriors Are." Armed with pitchforks, clubs, and other home-made weapons and singing the Hussite battle hymn, Ziska's peasant army on July 14, 1420 defeated a one hundred thousand man army of trained soldiers of the Emperor. The following year another army was sent by the Emperor and again Ziska's peasant army was triumphant. In 1422 still another army attacked Bohemia and despite losing his one good eye in battle, Ziska was still able to defeat the invaders. Though blind he continued to lead the Hussites for two more years until he was killed in battle in 1424. A former priest named Prokop took his place. Hussite soldier's, calling themselves "Ziska's Orphans" and despite being greatly out numbered, defeated an army of 130,000 that the Emperor and Pope sent to defeat them. The wars continued, and for fifteen years the Bohemian people were able to retain their independence from the Pope and the Empire. Great heroes and great battles became part of Bohemian national lore. The Emperor and Church concluded that they would never be able to defeat the Hussites by force so long as they remained united, so they embarked upon a strategy to divide them. The Ultaquists, who were a conservative branch of the Hussites, were primarily concerned about preserving Bohemian religious traditions within the Roman Church. The Taborites followed many of the more liberal teachings of Hus and Wycliffe. After extended negotiations Rome and the Ultaquists reached a compromise whereby the Ultraquists were allowed to continue worshipping in their own churches and were allowed to serve both wine and bread at communion. The conservative Ultraquists then joined forces with the army of Rome to defeat the army of the liberal Taborites at the battle of Lippan in 1434. Prokop and thirteen thousand Taborites were killed during the final battle. Bohemia was once again under the thumb of the Emperor and the Roman Church although it had achieved some degree of toleration for its unique religious traditions embodied in the services of the Ultraquists. For a while it seemed that Hus and all the casualties of the Hussite wars had died over a question of whether bread and wine or just bread would be served at communion. However, there were those who would not forget the more important reasons why Hus and the others had died.

Peter Chelchicky, a humble farmer, thought much about the bloodshed and destruction caused by the Hussite Wars. His reading of the Bible taught him, "Thou shalt not kill." He asked, "Why was all this killing going on in the name of God." Chelchicky concluded that the church liturgy, traditions and institutions that had developed over the years since the early Christian churches were founded by the apostles were not based on scripture. The Roman church was a man made institution like government, which was inspired by Satan not Christ. A Christian should faithfully follow the lessons of the Bible, as he in his own wisdom understood them, and should live a life like the early Christians. The church should become like the simple and primitive churches in the time of the apostles.

John Rokycana, the Ultraquist Archbishop of Prague, preached against the abuses of the Roman Church. When his nephew Gregory, a former monk, approached him about organizing a group of his friends who wanted to live their lives in accordance with true Christian principles, Rokycana referred Gregory and his friends to Chelchicky. After studying his writings and talking to him, they decided to establish a community based on his teachings. With the assistance of Rokycana, they secured permission from King George to form a Christian community on an estate surrounding the castle of Lititz near the village of Kunwald. They wrote to King George, "We are such who have for all time resolved to be guided only by the Gospel and by the pattern of the Lord Jesus Christ and the holy apostles in meekness, poverty, patience and love of enemies." As advocated by Chelchicky, they renounced the use of force and modeled their community on the practices of the early apostolic churches. The Bible was recognized as the only source of Christian belief. They sought to withdraw from the conflicts of the world. Calling themselves the Unitas Fratrum, which translates from the Latin as Unity of the Brethren, they formally organized in 1457. This date is considered the birth of the Moravian Church.

By 1461 the Brethren were perceived as heretics by the leaders of the Ultraquists and King George of Bohemia and persecution of the members began. Gregory was arrested along with others and tortured. He was laid upon the rack with his feet tied to a roller at one end and his hands to a roller at the other end. The purpose of the rack was to stretch the victim until he begged for mercy, confessed his heresy and recanted. If he did not, his arms and legs were pulled out of their sockets. Such were the methods of persuasion used at this time in history. Gregory refused to recant and was stretched until he passed out with pain. His uncle Rokycana rescued him and secured his release. Gregory was not the only one tortured. Many other members of the Brethren met the same fate. Four were burned at the stake. All were driven by soldiers from the estate where they had established their settlement. Their dream of a refuge where they would be left alone to follow Christ's teachings in peace was shattered, but their suffering did not destroy their faith and commitment. Like in the days of the early Christians, persecution only served to increase their faith and expand their following.

Since they were considered heretics by both the Roman church and the Ultraquists and therefore could not expect any assistance from the priests of either group, the Brethren took steps in 1464 to become an independent church. A secret synod was held in the mountains where a statement of faith was adopted and three elders elected as a governing board. In 1467 at another synod three ministers were elected. Since no Catholic or Ultraquist bishop would ordain their ministers, they were ordained by Bishop Stephen of the Waldensian Church, a small church which had survived independently of Rome, and which it was believed traced its origins to the apostolic church.

What was the Church of the Unity of the Brethren like in its early years? Services consisted of Bible reading, extemporoneous prayers from the heart, and plain Bible-based preaching by a minister without formal education who supported himself by his work not the collection plate. Congregational singing was important, and since there were no hymnbooks, the hymns were memorized. Church buildings were plain. In theology members believed Christians should not only obey the Ten Commandments but also Christ's teachings in the Sermon on the Mount. A Christian should not be angry or insulting, lust for a woman not his wife, divorce his wife, or swear to oaths. He should love his enemies, and if struck on the cheek, he should turn the other cheek. He should not spend his energies accumulating worldly treasures, but should commit himself to accumulating treasures in heaven. He should not practice his piety or pray in public in order to impress other people, and his gifts to the church should be private.[4] These were certainly not rules that most of the world lived by, and the Brethren saw themselves as living apart from the world. The congregation was considered a Christian community, which lived by rules of high moral conduct. Violations were punishable by exclusion from communion until there was sincere repentance. Living by a strict moral code did not mean they were unhappy. They felt the joy of receiving the magnificent gift of God's love and forgiveness, the assurance that each day of their lives was important to Him, and the hope that if they retained their faith and lived their lives in accordance with his teachings, they would join Him in Heaven. They did not fear suffering or death because they believed that Christ's followers were a special people who would suffer in this world and be rewarded in the next. The congregation was a caring community, which looked after the sick, the grieving, widows and orphans. Although Bible based, the Brethren did not believe in engaging in theological arguments. They did not believe there was one true church. They believed the essentials of the Christian faith are shared by all true believers regardless of the church which they attended.

At the beginning members were hostile to education and apprehensive about educated brethren. However, Bishop Luke, a graduate of the University of Prague, did much to

---

[4] These prescriptions are taken from Matthew, Chapters 5, 6 and 7, *Revised Standard Version of the Bible*.

change this thinking. He wrote a catechism for children, which was not only used for years by the Brethren, but also was translated and became widely circulated in Germany during the reformation. He also was instrumental in publication of the first hymnbook. He encouraged the services to become more liturgical and the buildings more attractive.

Students are taught that the Protestant reformation began with Martin Luther's "95 Theses", which attacked the Roman Church's practice of selling indulgences. He posted his protest on the castle church of Wittenberg in 1517. As noted above, Hus had spoken out against indulgences a hundred years before Luther and the organization that came to be known as the Moravian Church began sixty years before Luther began his efforts to organize a Protestant church in Germany. By 1517 the Unity of the Brethren, despite never being recognized as a lawful church in Bohemia and Moravia, had grown to about 200,000 members. Once they learned of Luther's efforts, the Brethren contacted and encouraged him. Luther recognized the Brethren as a Protestant church and gave it his blessing.

While the Protestants made great strides in northern Germany, Protestantism was severely repressed in Bohemia. King Ferdinand I of Bohemia defeated the Protestant King Frederick of Saxony at the battle of Muhlberg in 1547. Flush with victory he returned to Bohemia intent upon punishing the Protestants in his own country who had failed to support him. He ordered the Brethren to become Catholics or leave the country within six weeks. Several thousand left for neighboring Poland, and in a few years no less than forty congregations of Brethren had been established there. Many other Brethren remained in Bohemia seeking refuge on estates of sympathetic noblemen who did not strictly enforce the king's edict. As long as they did not attract the attention of hostile Catholics, they were allowed to remain.

During this time the Brethren's bishop John Augusta was arrested and tortured. He was smeared with pitch and set on fire. When this did not produce a confession of heresy, huge stones were piled on his body, and finally a hook was pierced through his flesh and he was hoisted up and suspended from the hook. When none of these tortures accomplished their desired result, he was imprisoned in a dark cell in a basement dungeon for sixteen years. Shortly before his death, King Ferdinand, perhaps desiring to make amends before he faced his Maker, set the old Bishop free.

The Church of Rome viewed the attacks of Luther, Calvin and the other reformers with alarm and vowed to defend and restore its ancient privileges. They found an ambitious political ally in the Hapsburgs, a royal family which controlled the thrones in much of the old Holy Roman Empire. The contest between the Protestants and Catholics for the soul and treasure of Europe was long and bloody. For several generations, Christians killed Christians in the name of God. The Thirty Years War raged from 1618 to 1648 and embroiled all of Europe in the struggle. Nowhere was the devastation worse than in Bohemia.

Although there were periods of toleration, the kings of Bohemia and Moravia were Catholic. Except for a brief period before the outbreak of the Thirty Years War, the Moravian Church was considered to be an illegal church. On July 6, 1609, King Rudolph in order to obtain the political support of the Protestants in a contest with his brother to preserve his throne signed a decree called the "Letter of Majesty" granting religious toleration to the Protestants. It included not only the Ultraquists but also for the first time the Brethren. Instead of meeting in private homes, they were permitted to worship at the Bethlehem Chapel at Prague where Hus had preached. By 1618 two thirds of the people of Bohemia were Protestant. This included Ultraquists and Lutherans and also members of the Unity of the Brethren. Many noblemen were members of the Brethren, and they were represented in the Council. This was the high point in the history of the ancient Brethren as a church organization. Most members no doubt believed that the future of their church was assured. Perhaps some lost the commitment and simple faith that the persecution and suffering of the early years had produced, and put their trust in promises of a worldly king and institutions of government.

The Catholic Church leadership in Bohemia and Rome did not accept the decision to open religion to competition. The contest came to a head over the right of Protestants to use church land for Protestant churches. Protestants had built their churches on church land and then protested when they were torn down by the Catholics. Protestants believed church land belonged to the King for church purposes and did not belong to the Church of Rome. The controversy reached a climax on May 23, 1618, at a stormy meeting of the Council when three representatives of the King were thrown out of the window of the Council Chambers. The incident was similar to that which occurred in 1419 and which had ignited the Hussite Wars. In this case the incident sparked the Thirty Years War which destroyed Bohemia and drove Protestants from the country.

At first the revolution seemed successful and the Protestants triumphant. The legislative assembly took over the government, expelled the Jesuits from the country, and the archbishop and other Catholic dignitaries left with them. Frederick, Elector of the Palatine and a Protestant, was chosen to be the new King of Bohemia in place of Ferdinand II, a member of the Hapsburg family and a Catholic. However, a Hapsburg army led by Ferdinand defeated Frederick's army at White Mountain near Prague on November 8, 1620. The defeat brought the Protestant revolution in Bohemia to an inglorious end. Ferdinand had twenty-seven members of the legislative assembly executed in the public square at Prague on June 21, 1621, a date that came to be known as the "Day of Blood." Fifteen of them were members of the Brethren. The edict of toleration was rescinded and the Roman Catholic Church was made the only lawful church in Bohemia and Moravia. Ferdinand achieved his goal of establishing a hereditary monarchy based on religious uniformity and divine right. He reestablished the old alliance in which the ruler protects the Church, and the Church provides legitimacy to the political power of the ruler.

The defeat of the Protestants at White Mountain did not bring peace. The great struggle by the Roman Church to reclaim what it had lost and the Hapsburgs to expand their dynasty continued until 1648. Ferdinand flush with his success over the Protestants in Bohemia now set his sights on Protestant kingdoms in Germany. His ambitions provoked others to enter the fray. The king of neighboring Saxony allied with the King of Sweden invaded Bohemia to thwart Ferdinand's ambitions. Spain, another Hapsburg kingdom, entered the war on the Catholic side. Bohemia remained a battleground in the contest for the soul of Europe for many years. The War finally ended with the Treaty of Westphalia in 1648. Under the Treaty the triumph of Catholicism in Bohemia was confirmed. As a result of the war and flight of Protestants from the country the population of Bohemia dropped from 3,000,000 to 800,000, and of the 150,000 landed families before the outbreak of war only 30,000 were left. Over 550 towns disappeared. Cities were depopulated and their houses left in ruins. Much of the national culture was destroyed. The Brethren fled to other countries to avoid persecution or went underground by hiding their beliefs. The Unity of Brethren no longer existed as a church organization in the land of its birth.

During this terrible time Bishop John Amos Comenius led the Brethren. In 1620 he was forced to flee from his home for safety. He was separated from his wife and children. His wife and daughter subsequently died of the plague. Comenius and a group of Brethren moved from place to place in

Bohemia for several years, and finally, unable to find any sanctuary within their own country, they set out for Poland. When Comenius reached the pass in the Giant Mountains during his flight from Bohemia, he knelt in the snow and lifted his hands in prayer. "May yet the merciful God not allow his word to perish in Bohemia with this exile, but may he leave behind a seed."[5] He would never again see his beloved homeland. Comenius escaped to Lissa, Poland where the Brethren had established an exile community. Despite the problems suffered by his church, Comenius became renowned throughout Europe as a pioneer of new methods in education. Among other reforms he introduced the picture book to help children learn to read and published an encyclopedia of useful knowledge. Comenius also became a leading advocate of unity among Protestants. He was open minded about different forms of worship, but preferred the simplicity of the early churches.

Misfortune was to strike Comenius and the Brethren again. For about twenty years they lived peacefully in Lissa, even establishing a college there that Comenius headed. Poland erupted in a War that included an invasion from the north and west by the Swedes under Protestant King Charles and an invasion from the east by the Russian Tsar's army. Austria intervened. Lissa was destroyed by fire in a battle between the Poles and the Swedes in 1656. Comenius' house, library, and other possessions were destroyed. This world-renowned scholar and educator once again was forced to flee for his life. With the defeat and withdrawal of the Swedish army came an end to toleration for the Brethren. Comenius received an invitation from a prominent citizen of Amsterdam promising a safe refuge that he was happy to accept. He spent the remainder of his life trying to assure that his Church would

---

[5] His words were later inscribed on the steeple of the Bohemian Church built in Berlin in 1736. John R. Weinlick and Albert H. Frank, *The Moravian Church through the Ages*, The Moravian Church in America, 1989, p. 40.

survive. Since the Brethren no longer had a homeland, he turned to English Christians for assistance. They provided money to publish Bohemian and Polish Bibles and to assist groups of Brethren to start churches in places where they had found refuge. Before he died Comenius published a history of the Brethren and an explanation of its teachings so that if exiles from Bohemia and Moravia were able to reestablish the church, they would have guidance. He died in 1670, at the age of seventy-eight, the Bishop of a church that to all appearances had disappeared.

During his lifetime Comenius saw his Church rise to its high point before the outbreak of the Thirty Years War. He then saw it destroyed in his homeland by the war and persecution of Protestants. He saw his church resurrected in Poland and then destroyed again by war and persecution. He saw his country savaged by years of war, depopulated, and reduced to a devastated frontier within the Hapsburg Empire centered in Vienna. He saw all of Europe torn asunder by armies fighting each other in the name of Christ. What was the effect on this scholarly, good-hearted man of God? A year before his death, he wrote that his theology was the Bible, his confession of faith was the Apostles' Creed, his prayer was the Ten Commandments. He acknowledged that sophisticated people of the world might think he was simply a foolish old man. But he had found Christ and that was everything to him. His whole life had been the journey of a pilgrim who had never found a city where he could abide in peace. He saw before him the heavenly fatherland to which Christ was leading him, and for him the one thing necessary was to forget the past and hasten to the prize which lay ahead.

When toleration returned to Poland, some of the Brethren went back and rebuilt the town of Lissa. In 1707 the town was again destroyed, this time by a Russian army. Many of the Polish Brethren joined the Reformed Church that had been organized in Poland. Only a few tiny congregations of the Brethren remained in Poland.

Some of the Moravians who did not flee from Bohemia and Moravia had gone underground. Careful to avoid detection by Jesuits searching for Protestants, they would meet at a home or in the woods where they would read from the Bohemian Bible, pray together, and sing hymns. Now and then they would receive a visit from a Brethren minister of a congregation outside the country with whom they would share communion. They were the "hidden seed" for which Comenius had prayed when he left the country. They were hidden from view but they preserved the beliefs of the Brethren until the time was right to sprout and grow into a church again.

The story of the ancient Unity of the Brethren is a story of people who for generations suffered severe persecution for their faith. They were driven from their homes and forced to live in the woods. They met secretly in each other's homes or in barns or fields. Frequently, they were forced to abandon their homes and seek refuge at the estate of a sympathetic nobleman or flee for safety to foreign lands. Many were thrown into cold, dark, filthy dungeons. Some were tortured on the rack, and others burned at the stake. Because of these terrible experiences, the Brethren's faith was considerably different from those of the Catholics or official state Protestant churches such as the Lutherans, Reformed, and Anglican, whose membership in church was required by law and custom. The Brethren viewed themselves as a small group of true believers who based their lives on the life of Christ and his disciples as revealed in the Scriptures. Just as Christ and many of his disciples suffered and died, they recognized their faith required the same of them if the occasion arose. As in the case of the early Christians, suffering did not diminish their faith; it fanned their faith to white-hot intensity. There was no place among them for people who wished to join simply because it was socially acceptable. Christianity began as a small group of believers persecuted for their faith, and the Brethren read their New Testaments and viewed themselves as following in the footsteps of their persecuted Savior and the apostles who created the first Christian churches.

CHAPTER 3

RENEWAL OF THE MORAVIAN CHURCH

The renewal of the Moravian Church dates from 1722 when Christian David, a carpenter and lay evangelist, persuaded Count Zinzendorf, a young Saxon nobleman, to allow a group of Moravians to settle on his estate in Silesia, a province of Saxony near Berthelsdorf. His estate became a refuge for Brethren seeking a place where they could practice their faith. Refugees came not only from Bohemia and Moravia, but also from other countries where they had fled to avoid persecution. In 1727 they organized themselves into the Renewed Unitas Fratrum or Unity of the Brethren, which came to be known as the Moravian Church because many of those who fled to Herrnhut came from Moravia.

Christian David, who persuaded Count Zinzendorf to allow the refugees to settle on his estate, was raised as a Catholic in Moravia and taught to hate Protestants with a passion. He came into contact with secret Protestants who impressed him with their courage and faith. He was troubled by the conflict between their views and the views of his Catholic friends and neighbors. He obtained a Bible and after reading it became concerned about what he had been taught in the Catholic Church. He became an itinerant carpenter so that he could visit Protestant countries and learn more about the

Protestant faith. After visiting various Protestant churches outside Moravia during his travels, he was disappointed to find that many Protestants were no better than Catholics. For a time he became disillusioned with religion. He joined the army hoping to find among soldiers facing death a higher morality. He was disappointed again and happy to be discharged. Traveling from place to place, he hoped to find someone who could make things clear. While at Goerlitz in Selesia, he became deathly ill, and for twenty weeks he was confined to bed. A kindly Lutheran minister, John Schwedler, visited him daily, cared for him, listened to the questions that troubled him, and helped him find answers. When he recovered, David joined Schwedler's church and married a member of his congregation. He found there the spirit of Christian fellowship and mutual assistance that he had been seeking so long.

Reverend Schwedler and his congregation were Pietists. Pietists believed traditional Lutherans placed too much emphasis on intellectual dogma and rituals. They felt the emphasis should be placed on the individual's conversion, belief in personal salvation, and pious living. To them Christianity should be a religion of the heart not a religion of the head.

Christian David felt called upon to share the joy that he received from his newfound faith. Remembering the Protestants back in Moravia, for five years he made secret trips searching for Protestants and preaching to them about the faith that he had discovered. He preached to plain men in a plain style with conviction. He spoke from the Bible with familiarity based on his years of study. His message inspired in his listeners hope and commitment, and they urged him to try to find a refuge for them in Silesia.

Count Zinzendorf was only 21 years old when he was persuaded by Christian David to allow the Moravian Protestants to come to his estate. David explained that the

Moravians were members of an ancient Protestant Church who despite years of persecution had held firm to their convictions and yearned for a place where they could practice their religion openly and live their lives in peace. John Roth, a good friend and Lutheran pastor, who the Count had installed as pastor of the village church on his estate, introduced the Count to David. Zinzendorf had recently purchased the estate from his grandmother, and he hoped with the assistance of Roth to establish on the estate a model Christian community.

The young Count's father had died when he was only six. His grandmother who was a devout Pietist raised him. When he was ten he was sent to a boarding school at Halle operated by a Pietist professor, and at sixteen at the insistence of his uncle he went to the University of Wittenberg to study law preparatory to a career in public service. Upon graduation he traveled throughout Europe to complete his education as a young nobleman. From an early age he had a close relationship with Christ and throughout his schooling and travels pursued religious studies with a passionate interest. Being familiar with the ideas of Luther and the Pietists, he came to believe strongly that most of the differences between the Protestants were unimportant.

Upon learning of the Count's willingness to accept the Moravian refugees, David returned to Moravia and informed the Niesser family at Sehlen of the Count's decision. The family and a few relatives abandoned their possessions and set out with David across the mountains to the Count's estate. When they arrived two weeks later, the Count was not there. His steward found a location for them to settle a mile from the village. He called the place "Herrnhut" which means the Lord's Watch. Soon the first house was built and others were under construction. David was to make nine more trips to Moravia bringing back emigrants. Word spread of the new community and many found their way there. Initially all were enthused with the excitement of creating a new Christian community.

During the first few years after the settlement of Hernnhut, differences arose among the members because of their diverse backgrounds, lack of organization, and theological differences. The settlement had attracted some religious dissidents not connected with the Unity of the Brethren who stirred up religious discord. Count Zinzendorf, who worked for the government in Dresden, did not pay much attention to the residents of Herrnhut at first. When he discovered that problems had developed at the village, he took a leave of absence from his official duties to apply his ideas to the challenge of saving the community from disintegration. As landlord he summoned them all to appear and spoke to them on the dangers of schisms. He then produced a list of rules which all must obey if they were to remain on his estate. The rules were based on the customs of a typical German village of the time. Their duties as members of the community were made clear. Through discussions with them he developed another agreement entitled "The Brotherly Union and Compact" which was a statement of the beliefs that they shared and the commitments that they were willing to make. Only those who were willing to sign the Agreement could live at Herrnhut. The agreement organized them as a society within the Lutheran Church. As a nobleman trained in the law and a Lutheran, he required them to attend the Lutheran Church in the nearby village. The Lutheran Church was the recognized church of Saxony. In accordance with Pietist teaching, he asked them to think of themselves as a "church within a church." The Count talked with all of them and encouraged them to talk to each other. The divisions that previously separated them disappeared. As he learned more about them, he became interested in the history of the Brethren and discovered the writings of Comenius on the Brethren's discipline and history and his hopes for its renewal. He was astonished to find how similar his rules were to the discipline outlined by Comenius. He shared with them what he had learned about the ancient church. On August 13, 1727, the members of the Hernnhut community joined in a celebration of the Holy Communion at Pastor Roth's village church and experienced a powerful spiritual rebirth that overcame their prior differences and bound them together into a united community of committed believers. The service was followed by a "love feast" where all shared a meal together as the apostles had done. The Moravian Church considers this the date when the ancient Unity of the Brethren was renewed and celebrates it annually.

During the next five years, Herrnhut developed into a communal Christian community in which religious, economic, and civic life were organized into an integrated whole. The community was divided into groups called choirs based on age, gender, and marital status. This was done partly for reasons of economy, partly because the needs of each group were different, and partly because such groups developed strong bonds of fellowship and mutual assistance. Everyone worked for Christ. The work of the village was carefully organized to assure that everyone's effort contributed to a need of the village. Cooperation was assured and wasteful competition avoided. Villagers worked hard because work was a sacred duty, a joy, and necessary for the welfare of the community. The products of farm, handicraft, and shops supplied not only the needs of the community, but provided a surplus that was used to fund missionary and evangelical work. Single men were assigned to the single brethren's house where they lived, worked, and worshipped together. Apprentices worked under masters to assure that they developed skills. Single women lived in the single sister's house, and worked on handicrafts and childcare. Married couples lived in a separate house. Widows had a house and so did children who were not living with their parents. Those who because of age, injury or sickness could not care for themselves were taken care of by the community. The day began and ended with a service of hymn singing and prayer. Prayer was conducted around the clock with each hour of the day and night assigned to a man and woman. Each day a verse of Scripture was handed out to think about and provide inspiration.

Unlike some other religious communities, Herrnhut was not organized around a strong, charismatic, dictatorial leader. Authority over secular affairs was lodged in a town meeting, and authority over religious affairs in a church council and board of elders. Although the Count was influential, his influence was through his wisdom and persuasiveness, not his economic power or administrative abilities. The Moravians also followed the Biblical example of using the lot to decide questions where there was not unanimous agreement. They believed that by so doing they were allowing God to make the decision. This belief and practice also avoided the dissension that has so often torn apart other religious communities. An important example of this is the question of whether the Moravians should drop their ancient traditions and practices and become fully integrated into the Lutheran Church. This was advocated by the Count at one time and opposed by the Moravians. The question was submitted to the lot and decided in favor of remaining separate.

The focus of the religious experience for those at Herrnhut was feeling the presence of Christ in their daily lives. They felt his presence in everything they did. Although they believed the Bible was the only authoritative source for Christian belief, they felt a unity with all Christians regardless of denomination who believed in Christ and felt his presence. This essential unity made denominational differences in ritual and theology unimportant. Unlike other Protestant churches at the time they refused to become involved in theological disputes about interpretations of Scripture.

The Renewed Church was evangelical. Members were encouraged to discuss their spiritual life with each other in small groups. Services were emotional and powerful. Singing and instrumental music were important parts of worship. The love feast, which included the sharing of food and beverage during a service, was introduced as a means of sharing Christian love. Members were fired with a desire to share their religious experience with others, and to bring the message of Christ's love to those who had never experienced Christianity.

In this age of terrorists and violent revolutionaries, it is difficult to think of the meek and gentle Jesus as a revolutionary. How could someone who taught love, compassion, and forgiveness be a revolutionary? Yet was there anyone who has had more impact on the history of the world? The Moravians at Herrnhut were also meek and gentle people. Who would think of these peace-loving, long-sufffering, compassionate people as revolutionaries? Yet revolutionary ideas came out of the evangelical spirit at Herrnhut. The first they called diaspora, and today is non-denominational evangelism. Count Zinzendorf believed strongly in the unity of all true Christians. It made no difference what denomination they were. Evangelists spread out across Europe from Herrnhut. They were not seeking new members for the Moravian Church. They were seeking to bring nonbelievers to Christ and revive the faith of members of other denominations whose faith had lapsed. They encouraged converts who were members of existing churches to remain members of the denominations in which they had grown up. The goal was to bring people to Christ and to encourage believers to share the experience of their faith. A convert could remain a member of his or her Lutheran Church in Germany, Reformed Church in Switzerland, or the Church of England, and at the same time meet together with a small group of other believers to share and nourish each other's faith. Meeting in each other's houses, a passage from Scripture would be read, a hymn sung, a prayer said by someone who was moved to speak, and a religious experience or question shared and discussed. Members of the group were still expected to attend the services of their respective church.

In the present age of religious toleration and ecumenical churches, the Moravians idea about the unity of all Christians seems common place. At that time the idea was revolutionary and threatening. Religious leaders maintained positions of power and influence by convincing political leaders and common people that their religion was the only true religion and that members of other denominations were heretics. Lutheran ministers in Germany, Ministers of the Reformed Church in Switzerland, or Ministers of the Church of England could be every bit as dogmatic and cruel as Catholic priests. The shepherds retained their flock by teaching their sheep to hate the shepherd and sheep in the other flock. Therefore, for the Moravians to travel around Europe telling people that it really made no difference what denomination you belonged to, that all good Christians shared the same core belief and that the different rituals and Scriptural interpretation in the different denominations was really not important was dangerous in eighteenth century Europe. Millions of people had been tortured and lost their homes, possessions and even their lives in wars during the past two centuries fighting over which ritual and doctrine was the true religion.

Revolutionaries make enemies because they threaten the status of the powerful. A revolutionary idea is particularly dangerous when it attacks the legitimacy of their power. The more dangerous a revolutionary is, the more he is hated and attacked. Jesus was dangerous to the High Priests of Jerusalem, so they hated him and had him killed. Hus was dangerous to the Pope and the Cardinals, so they hated him and had him killed. The ideas of the Count and the Moravians were dangerous to the leaders of the Lutheran Church in Saxony and leaders of other establishment Protestant churches in Europe, so they hated and attacked them. The Count was accused of harboring heretics and fomenting peculiar religious ideas at Herrnhut. In 1832 an offical commission was sent from Dresden to investigate the charge. They attended services and interviewed residents of the community. Upon receipt of the commision's report an edict was issued finding that the Moravians should be allowed to remain so long as they behaved themselves quietly. The Count considered this a threat which was intended to silence him and them. The edict also ordered that the Schwenkfelders, another Protestant sect that had taken refuge on the Count's estate, must leave Saxony. In 1836 following another investigation the King banished the Count from Saxony on the grounds that he was guilty of heresy. The Moravians were allowed to remain at Herrnhut, but they were forbidden to admit new members. The attacks on him in his own country prompted the Count to establish new communties outside Saxony. Communities like Herrhnut were established in Prussia known as Herrnhag and Marienborn. Another community was established in Holland called Heerendyk. The attacks also caused the Count and Moravians to focus their efforts on missionary work outside Europe.

The Moravians at Herrnhut had another revolutionary idea. They felt strongly that it was the duty of Christians to bring the Christian message to peoples who had never heard of Christ's teachings. Although this idea seems unremarkable today, at the time it also was revolutionary among Protestant churches. None of the established Protestant Churches of Europe had missionary programs at that time. This is not to say that some governments did not sponsor missionary work, or that there were not private groups who sponsored missionaries or individual Christians who felt the call.

However, missionary work was simply not considered a responsibility of the established Protestant churches. Therefore, when the Moravians accepted missionary work as a primary responsibility of their church, they were once again ahead of their time.

One of the reasons many European Christians were not interested in missionary work was their sense of racial and cultural superiority. They really did not believe the native populations in the lands the Europeans had conquered were God's children and just as eligible as white Europeans to go to Heaven. What sort of place was Heaven if black Africans, red Indians, brown Arabs, and yellow Chinese were there? The common European belief that natives were not God's children was also the reason why it was perfectly all right for Europeans to murder, torture and enslave them and steal their lands and possessions. The Moravians believed that all people were God's children and capable of salvation, and this was revolutionary and threatening.

The Moravian's idea as to how missionaries should go about their work was also revolutionary. They believed they should not be a burden on the people with whom they lived. Therefore, they must have a trade so that they could be self-supporting. They were trained in the Bible, languages, geography and practical medicine. They were to live humbly among the natives and not dominate them. Teaching was to focus on the crucified Christ as personal Lord and Savior, not the finer points of religious theology. They were not to try to convert the nation; they were to focus on individual conversions. Once a few natives were converted, the converts would assist in bringing others to Christ.

The first missionaries left Herrnhut in 1732 for St. Thomas in the West Indies to work among the plantation slaves. St. Thomas was a colony of Denmark. In 1731 while attending the coronation of the new King of Denmark, the Count met a slave who spoke to him of the hard and bitter lives of the slaves on St. Thomas. He stated that his brother and sister yearned to hear about Christ. When the Count returned to Herrnhut, he related what he heard to the congregation. Two young men felt called to go to the island, and asked the Count for permission. When the Count informed the congregation of the request, many opposed the request, feeling that they were simply being young and foolish. The requests were submitted to the lot and decided in favor of one and against the other.

Another man was chosen to go along to help the young man get started and after a period of training the two set out for Denmark. The Danish West Indies Company at first wanted nothing to do with the missionaries, but soon they won over the Queen and other members of the Royal household, and were on their way to the Island. When they arrived, they discovered there were about 3,000 black slaves on the island and only 300 planters. The planters maintained their control by cruelty, which kept the slaves in fear. For the first offense, a slave was whipped, for a second his ears were chopped off, and for a third his head was cut off and hung on a post along the road as a warning to others. Slaves were forbidden to marry. As a result of this treatment, slaves did not trust white men, including white missionaries. Although some were supportive, many planters were hostile to the missionary effort believing that it would interfere with their control over the slaves. The tropical climate and bad water were also a challenge to the missionaries' health. Additional missionaries were sent to help. The Count himself visited the Island, and when he arrived he found the missionaries in jail accused of not having the proper authority to administer baptisms. He convinced the governor to free the missionaries, held open-air meetings throughout the island for three weeks, and by the time he left was able to announce that the message was being preached at fifty plantations.

In the first few years of the mission at St. Thomas twenty-one of twenty-nine missionaries sent there died of illness. They did not die in vain. Thousands of plantation slaves found Christ, and chapels and schools were built throughout the island. As a result of the work on St. Thomas, missions were subsequently sent to other islands in the West Indies: St. Croix in 1734, St. John in 1741, Jamaica in 1754, Antigua in 1756, Barbados in 1765, St. Kitts in 1777, and Tobago in 1790. The work on all these islands was begun among plantation slaves.

In 1733 another group of missionaries left for Greenland to work among the Eskimos. In 1735 missionaries went to Surinam in South America and Georgia in North America. In 1737 missionary work began in South Africa, Ceylon, and Guinea.

CHAPTER 4

MISSIONS IN AMERICA

The first Moravian missionaries to settle in America embarked from London on January 23, 1735, and arrived at Savannah, Georgia, on April 6, 1735. Ten men were led by August Spangenberg, Count Zinzendorf's assistant. Following the example of Hernnhut, they commenced construction of a self-supporting religious community near Savannah that would serve as a base for missionary work among the Creeks, Cherokees and other Indian tribes in the area.

The Moravian missionaries were among the early settlers of Georgia. Under the leadership of James Oglethorpe, a prominent soldier and statesman, a charity was organized and granted a charter for the territory below the English colony of South Carolina and above Florida that was then claimed by Spain. The purpose of the charity was to raise money to send persons who had been imprisoned for debt to Georgia. This was to afford them an opportunity through work in the colony to make something of themselves, and it would relieve the British government of the cost of imprisoning them in England. The charity would also pay the way for Protestant refugees from Europe who were escaping from persecution in their homelands. Since England was a Protestant state, it became a refuge for many Protestants escaping persecution on the mainland of Europe. The Protestant refugees were a financial burden for England, and part of the charity's purpose was to provide a place in the colony for them. More substantial settlers would also be encouraged to settle, but they would have to pay their own way. Between 1733 and 1742 the charity underwrote the cost of shipping 1,847 persons to Georgia, of which 839 were foreign Protestants, and the rest indigent Britons. In addition there were an additional 1,304 who paid their own way to the colony. Apart from providing a refuge for indigents and Protestants refugees, another goal of the charity was to bring Christianity to the Indians. Oglethorpe had led the first group of settlers to Georgia and had begun construction of Savannah in early 1733, only two years before the Moravian missionaries arrived.

The first group of Protestant refugees to be given passage to Georgia was called the Salzbergers, and they arrived in 1734. Having learned about the Salzbergers, Count Zinzendorf contacted the Trustees on behalf of the Schwenkfelders who had been ordered out of Saxony. They had found a temporary refuge at Herrnhut, but had been ordered to leave. The Count was successful in persuading Oglethorpe's group to transport them to Georgia. They set out for England, but upon arriving in Holland, they were persuaded to change their destination to Pennsylvania. A Moravian went along to assist them. The Count's efforts on behalf of the Schwenkfelders then prompted discussion of a Moravian mission to Georgia. At the time Zinzendorf and the Herrnhut community were under attack from enemies in Saxony so their interest in Georgia was also prompted by anxiety over whether they would be allowed to remain in Saxony. If they were ordered to leave, they could seek refuge in the new world. At that time America was the great sanctuary for religious refugees from Europe.

The first ten Moravians arrived in London under the leadership of August Spangenberg, the Count's assistant who had abandoned an academic career to join him at Herrnhut.

When they arrived in London with no money for their passage to Georgia, they met with Oglethorpe and the other Trustees who were quite impressed by their story and commitment. The Trustees agreed to give them two lots in Savannah and two fifty acre tracts which were divided into five acre gardens close to town and forty-five acre farms further out. They also set aside 500 acres for the Count if he chose to locate there. The Trustees agreed to loan the Moravians the money for their passage.

The journey from London to Georgia took nine weeks. The Moravians soon endeared themselves to a group of Swiss who were on the boat as well as the crew. They helped the crew with their tasks without request for compensation and tended to the needs of the Swiss who were sick. Upon arrival at Savannah they quickly erected a twenty by ten foot cabin on one of the town lots that they all shared and began planting their garden and clearing one of their farm tracts. They also took jobs assisting with construction to earn money. They needed to become self-supporting before their missionary work could begin.

The Moravians quickly established friendly relations with the Salzbergers who shared a common language and religious convictions. Their relations with the English colonists in Savannah were cordial but difficult because the Moravians did not speak English, and the English did not share the Moravians interest in religion. A nearby tribe of Indians was friendly and enjoyed the Moravians hospitality and their singing, but the language barrier prevented more meaningful contact. The Moravians sought to overcome the language barrier by hiring an English maid and taking charge of an English orphan boy from whom they learned to speak. A few of them began learning the language of the nearby tribe. Although the Moravians had informed Oglethorpe that they could not bear arms, and he agreed to respect their sentiments, there was nothing in writing. The Moravians entered into an agreement with Oglethorpe's local magistrate whereby they were allowed to pay for two substitutes to perform their share of the town watch.

A second company of twenty-five Moravians left London on October 14, 1735, and arrived at Savannah on February 23, 1736, under the leadership of Bishop David Nitschmann. Nitschman had been made a Bishop so he could ordain ministers in the new world. Among the passengers on the ship were James Oglethorpe, leader of the Colony, and John and Charles Wesley, who subsequently founded the Methodist Church. John Wesley, then an impressionable young man, recorded in his journal the following incident concerning the Moravians:

> The waves of the sea were mighty, and raged horribly. They rose up to the heavens above, and clave down to hell beneath. The winds roared round about us, and - what I never heard before - whistled as distinctly as if it had been a human voice. The ship not only rocked to and fro with the utmost violence, but shook and jarred with so unequal, grating a motion, that one could not but with great difficulty keep one's hold on anything, or stand a moment without it. Every ten minutes came a shock against the stern or side of the ship, which one would think would dash the planks in a thousand pieces.... At seven I went to the Germans. I had long before observed the great seriousness of their behavior Of their humility they had given a continual proof, by performing those servile offices for the other passengers, which none of the English would undertake; for which they desired, and would receive no pay, saying "It was good for their proud hearts," and "their loving Saviour had done more for them." And every day had given them occasion of showing a meekness, which no injury could move. If they were

pushed, struck, or thrown down, they rose again and went away; but no complaint was found in their mouth. There was now an opportunity of trying whether they were delivered from the spirit of fear, as well as from that of pride, anger and revenge. In the midst of the psalm wherewith their service began, wherein were mentioning the power of God, the sea broke over, split the mainsail in pieces, covered the ship, and poured in between the decks, as if the great deep had already swallowed us up. A terrible screaming began among the English. The Germans looked up, and without intermission calmly sang on. I asked one of them afterwards, "Were you not afraid?" He answered, "I thank God, no." I asked, "But were not your women and children afraid?" He replied mildly, "No, our women and children are not afraid to die." From them I went to their crying, trembling neighbors, and found myself enabled to speak with them in boldness and to point out to them the difference in the hour of trial between him that feareth God and him that feareth him not. At twelve the wind fell. This was the most glorious day which I had hitherto seen.[6]

John Wesley's experience with the Moravians did not end with the trip. While living in Savannah, he had many conversations with the Moravians and observed their services. His experience made him admire their simple faith. He even inquired about becoming a communicant member of their Church. The Moravians politely declined on the ground that he did not know them well enough, and they did not know him well enough. This was consistent with their practice of

---

[6] This passage from Wesley's diary is cited in Adelaide Fries, *Moravians in Georgia 1735-1740*, Edwards & Broughton, Raleigh, N.C. 1905, Chapter 4

admitting communicant members only after both the member and congregation were sure that the decision had been very carefully considered, and the member was ready to commit to the discipline of the group. Upon return to England Wesley met regularly with a group of Moravians in London, and during this time period both he and his brother experienced what they both described as their conversion, in modern evangelical terms, their rebirth in Christ or "born again" experience. John Wesley then visited Count Zinzendorf and the Moravian communities of Herrnhag and Herrnhut. Although he differed from the Moravians in some respects, the Moravians had a considerable influence on John Wesley and the early history of the Methodist Church. From the Moravians came the Methodists' evangelical spirit and zeal that characterized that church in its early years.

Illness, brought on by the hot, steamy weather, and diseases fomenting in the swamps and river bottoms, made many of the Moravians ill and several died. However, the final blow to the Georgia mission was an issue of conscience. Problems developed with the Spanish in 1737. The Spanish occupied Florida at the time and looked with alarm on the British settlements in Georgia. They threatened to invade. Both sides enlisted the aid of Indian tribes to fight for them. The residents of Savannah were frequently fearful of attack by Spanish soldiers or their Indian allies. Oglethorpe's town magistrate insisted that all men be prepared to fight. The Moravians insisted that they could not bear arms. Then the towns people took up the cry. Why should they fight for these strangers who would not do their share toward defending the land? They would kill them first. As so often is the case, the anxiety of war caused the towns people to search for an enemy within the town. The Moravians became the object of their hatred and scorn. The Moravians' appeal to Oglethorpe was denied. They must provide two men for military duty, and they were denied permission to carry on their missionary work

42

with Indians unless they performed their military duty as citizens. If they chose not to comply, they were granted permission to leave the colony. By 1740, most of them had left for Pennsylvania. They left behind the buildings and cleared fields that had cost them so much effort.

The Moravians had come to America to establish a mission among the Indians. Their first attempt in Georgia failed to accomplish this objective. Although they did succeed in opening a school for children in an Indian village several miles from Savannah, the tensions between the Spanish and English and their Indian allies had made it dangerous to pursue further missionary work in Georgia. Although the Georgia mission did not succeed, the Moravians did not abandon their goal of establishing a community in America that could serve as a base for missionary work. The effort in Georgia provided the foundation for the establishment of such a community in Pennsylvania. Many from the Georgia community became the founders of Bethlehem, Pennsylvania.

It is not surprising that the Georgia Moravians would end up in Pennsylvania. William Penn established the colony for religious refugees. Although his particular interest was Quakers who were persecuted in England, all Christian faiths were welcome. As a result, 18th century Pennsylvania included a wide variety of Protestant religious sects. Also Penn encouraged German-speaking people to settle in Pennsylvania. Because Germany as a nation did not exist during the American colonial period, the Dutch, as they were called, included people from a number of kingdoms and principalities, which later became part of Germany. The Dutch also included German-speaking people from Switzerland, France, and Holland. In 1775 the Dutch made up approximately one-third of the population of the state. They were a higher percentage in frontier counties including Northampton and Lancaster Counties where the Moravians settled.

George Whitefield, a Methodist evangelist from England, who was in Georgia when the last of the Moravians decided to leave, offered to take them to Pennsylvania on his boat. This was the year of what has been called "The Great Awakening." Whitefield, who was perhaps one of the best evangelical preachers that the world has ever produced, preached to large crowds in the middle colonies and New England. He even preached to large crowds of German-speaking people, and in this Peter Boehler, a Moravian preacher aided him. A religious revival swept the colonies. Whitefield's approach usually included a solicitation for donations to a worthy cause. One of his causes was a school for black children. He had acquired a large tract of land in Pennsylvania for this purpose. He asked the Moravians if they would develop and operate the school for him, which they readily agreed to do. A doctrinal dispute later arose between him and the Moravians. Whitefield canceled the agreement to sell the Moravians the land even though they had begun work on the first building. The Moravians bought another tract nearby. Whitefield then agreed to sell them his land as well. On these tracts the Moravians developed communities that they named Bethlehem and Nazareth.

The two communities were in what is now Northampton County, Pennsylvania. This county is located west of the Delaware River just north of Bucks County, about 60 miles north of Philadelphia. The communities were south of the Blue Mountains. They were on the frontier, and in fact a Indian village was located on one of the tracts at the time of its purchase.

Count Zinzendorf arrived in New York on November 30, 1741. After a brief stay, he set out for the new settlement to spend Christmas with the Moravians who had just completed the first building there. They celebrated a joyous holy communion together in a log building which had been constructed on the site where they planned to construct the

44

Hermnhut of the new world. Attached to it was a barn where the horses and cows could be heard. The Count reminded all that Jesus was born in a stable among the animals in the village of Bethlehem and proposed that they name their new village Bethlehem. In addition to Bethlehem, the Count organized Moravian congregations at Philadelphia, Germantown, Falkner's Swamp, Oley, and Nazareth during his two-year visit to America. The principal purpose of the Count's visit was not to organize Moravian congregations. After leading the first group of Moravians to Georgia, Spangenberg had gone to Pennsylvania in 1736 to work with the Schwenkfelders who the Moravians had assisted after they were ordered out of Saxony. They had been given refuge at Hermnhut, and the Count had found a refuge for them in Georgia. They decided to go to Pennsylvania instead, and a Moravian had accompanied them there. Spangenberg hoped to persuade them to join with the Moravians in establishing a community in Pennsylvania. Although they welcomed his assistance in organizing their own community, the Schwenkfelders were unwilling to join with the Moravians. Spangenberg reported to the Count that Pennsylvania, which was established by William Penn, as a land of religious toleration and refuge for persecuted Christians, had become a hotbed of competing, quarrelling religious sects. The religious freedom that they experienced encouraged each to pursue its particular view of the truth. Frequently, they competed for members by calling each other names and attacking each other's theology. At the same time a large part of the population had entirely abandoned religion. For the Count the situation was ripe for the application of his ideas concerning the essential unity of all Christians. He proposed to establish a "Congregation of God in the Spirit" which would bring all the quarrelling groups together so that they could concentrate their efforts on those who had no faith. The project was to be achieved by a series of synods to which the different denominations would send representatives. Together they would strive to identify their core beliefs and promote the spirit that bound them all together as Christians. The first synod was well attended, but with time more and more of the groups dropped out so that finally the synods were simply gatherings of Moravians. The Count spent considerable time and effort to make the synods a success, but many of the groups became suspicious of the Count's motives and apprehensive that his efforts threatened their own plans. As in Europe he and the Moravians became the objects of vilification and personal attacks by leaders of other religious groups who felt threatened by their ecumenical message. The Count's ideas were revolutionary and brought the customary reaction by those who felt their power threatened.

Another goal of the Count's visit to America was to energize and organize the missionary program. He visited the mission that had been started by Christian Henry Rauch at Shekomeko, New York in 1740, and participated in the organization of the first Indian congregation there in 1742. Spangenberg had become a friend of Conrad Weiser, who lived 70 miles west of Philadelphia. A friend of the Indians, Weiser served as interpreter for the Penns and was the most knowledgeable man in the colony on Indian affairs. With the assistance of Weiser, the Count made three journeys to the Indian country beyond the Blue Mountains to meet with tribal chiefs. A treaty of friendship was made with the Iroquois Confederation, known as the Six Nations, which controlled most of the land outside the area of white settlement in the northeastern United States.

One of the Count's visits was to a Shawnee town in the Wyoming valley of Pennsylvania where he explained the purpose of his visit was to teach them about the Savior. He and his little group pitched their tents on the banks of the Susquehanna, a little below the town. His visit caused alarm among the Shawnee who concluded that his real motive, like other whites, was to acquire their land. It appeared highly unlikely to them that a stranger should cross the ocean from his home in Europe for the sole purpose of instructing them on the means of obtaining happiness after death, asking for nothing in return. They decided to murder him and to do it quietly so as not to provoke a war with the English. According to one account the following occurred:

Zinzendorf was alone in his tent, seated upon a bundle of dry weeds, which composed his bed, and engaged in writing, when his assassins approached to execute their bloody mission. It was night and the cool air of September had rendered a small fire necessary to his comfort and convenience. A curtain formed of blanket and hung upon pins was the only guard to the entrance of the tent. The heat of the small fire had roused a large rattlesnake that lay in the weeds not far from it; and the reptile to enjoy it more effectually, crawled slowly into the tent and passed over one of his legs undiscovered. Without, all was still and quiet, except the gentle murmur of the river at the rapids, a mile below. At this moment the Indians softly approached the door of his tent, and lightly removed the curtain, contemplated the venerable man too deeply engaged in the subject of his thoughts to notice either their approach or the snake that extended before him. At a sight like this, even the heart of the savage shrunk from the idea of committing so horrid an act, and quitting the spot, they hastily returned to the town and informed their companions that the Great Spirit protected the white man, for they had found him with no door but a blanket, and had seen a large rattlesnake crawl over his legs without attempting to injure him.[7]

---

[7] I. Daniel Rupp, *History of Lancaster County*, 1844, pp. 283-284.

Following this incident he was able to win their friendship and confidence and spent twenty days with them before returning to Bethlehem. Zinzendorf returned to Europe in January 1743.

In June 1742, Bethlehem and Nazareth were organized into a new kind of Moravian community. Although the experience at Herrnhut provided the source for many ideas used in those communities, they were organized to achieve the goal of supporting the missionary program of the Moravians in America and to address the special challenges presented by that undertaking. At the meeting in June, the residents of the village were divided into two companies, one with responsibility for the missionary effort and the other with responsibility to operate the home base that supported the missionary work. The responsibility for administering the villages was assigned to August Spangenberg. He was not only committed, he possessed the necessary administrative skills. Spangenberg established and organized what was called the "General Economy." The success of the plan was based on the commitment of the members of the communities to contribute their work in exchange for food and shelter, but no wages or payment for what they produced. Each worked for Christ and the good of the community. Each received what they needed and the surplus supported the missionaries. They lived by the motto, "Together we pray, together we labour, together we suffer, together we rejoice." In these deeply religious communities, work was a joy because it was God's work. Each felt that their effort was an important contribution to the work that they as a community of believers were doing for Christ. No one was required to stay, but in order to remain in the community one had to do his or her share of the work.

The missionary effort of the Moravians was not simply the work of the missionaries in the field. It was also the work of the farmers who produced the grains and the meat that supported the community, the artisans who made products for the use of the community or to be sold to provide money for the missionary effort, the carpenters and other craftsmen who built the houses and mills, the women who made the clothes for the community and tended the children. They were all missionaries because the purpose of the community was to support the missionaries, and they all contributed their skills and labor to make it happen.

By 1762 the community had sufficiently progressed so that the General Economy could be abandoned and residents could each own their own trade or business or work for wages, but this did not mean that the purpose of the community had changed. The communities still considered it their responsibility to support the mission program. Moravian communities were later developed on the same model at Lititz in Pennsylvania; Hope in New Jersey, and Salem in North Carolina. Bethlehem became the center of the church's activities in the north and Salem became the center in the south.

Lord Granville offered to sell the Moravians 100,000 acres in North Carolina. In 1752 August Spangenberg was sent to the colony to locate a suitable tract. Since such a large tract could not be located along the coast, Spangenberg and his party went west to see what could be found. They came upon a vast area of open land at the three forks of Muddy Creek, which Spangenberg decided was suitable. He called the tract Wachau because it reminded him of Wachau, Austria. Settlers later changed the name to Wachovia. On August 7, 1753, the land was conveyed to the Moravian Church by the proprietors of the colony.

The first settlers came from Bethlehem. On October 8, 1753, fifteen men left Bethlehem with a wagon full of provisions. On November 17 they arrived at the Moravian tract and found an abandoned log cabin that they repaired, and additional cabins were built. The first village that the Moravians established at Wachovia was named Bethabara. In

1759 a second village was established three miles from Bethabara named Bethania. In 1765 the Moravians began work on Salem that was to be the principal Moravian town at Wachovia. In 1772 it was completed and many of the Moravians from the other villages moved there. It resembled a small German town in the middle of the American frontier.

Like Bethlehem and Nazareth in Pennsylvania and the mother church at Herrnhut, Saxony, the Moravian villages at Wachovia were organized so that economic, social, and religious life were all integrated around the church. The church owned the land and buildings and everyone worked for the church and leased their house from the church. Men and women were organized into choirs based on age, gender and marital status with their own buildings and activities. The communities had skilled craftsmen and a church store that made them the trading center for western North Carolina. The quality of the goods that they manufactured was renowned throughout the colonies.

There were many German-speaking people in Wachovia who were not Moravians. Many of them had their children baptized in the Moravian Church and even attended services at a Moravian Church, but they were not communicant members. In accordance with their practice in Pennsylvania and Europe, the church held services that the public could attend. However, only communicant members were permitted to attend communion services. For a Moravian participation in Holy Communion was a high privilege and emotionally charged experience reserved only for true believers who had committed themselves to Christ. Becoming a communicant member, and thus entitled to participate in Holy Communion, was a very important event both for the member and the church, not to be undertaken lightly. It usually was preceded by a significant period of soul-searching. As mentioned earlier, John Wesley was not considered ready to become a communicant member by the Moravians in

Georgia. It was not unusual for a family to include communicant and non-communicant members.

The Moravian communities in Pennsylvania and North Carolina were to provide a base of operations for the Moravian's missionary work among the Indians in the north and the south. In each case they started with nothing but a tract of land in the wilderness and through incredibly hard work and personal sacrifice created thriving little German communities which contrasted sharply with the rough frontier communities which surrounded them. The residents' lives revolved around their work and the religious services that began and ended each day. They were gentle, humble, nonviolent, kind people who were fair in all their dealings. The frontier culture that surrounded them was assertive, boastful, crude, suspicious, and violent. The Moravians were communal and highly disciplined, sacrificing personal interests for the good of the community. Frontier culture was highly individualistic and undisciplined. Excessive drinking was an accepted part of the social fabric of frontier life and was not tolerated within Moravian communities. A high percentage of the families on the frontier had no association with any church whereas church services and activities were a central part of Moravian community life. Frontier children frequently had no schooling while the Moravians always provided schooling for the children of their communities. Living on the frontier was dangerous not only because of danger from hostile Indians, but also from the unprincipled characters who were attracted to the frontier because of the absence of legal and social constraints. The question was whether the Moravian communities could survive in such a hostile environment, and if so, could they accomplish their goal of supporting an effective missionary program.

The Moravians first mission among the Indians began in 1740 with the efforts of Christian Heinrich Rauch at Shekomeko among the Mohicans in what is now the Town of

51

Pine Plains, Dutchess County, New York, about 30 miles southwest of Stockbridge. Christian Henry Rauch arrived in New York in July, 1740, and accepted an invitation of Chiefs Tschoop and Shabash of the Mohicans to come to Dutchess County. The two chiefs were converted to Christianity.

How this came about was later described by Chief Tschoop at a conference in Bethlehem. It was then retold in the following colorful story as a lesson for other missionaries. Chief Tschoop is reputed to have said the following:

> I have been a heathen, and grown old among the heathen; therefore I know how the heathen think. Once a preacher came and began to explain that there was a God. We answered, 'Dost thou think us so ignorant as not to know that? Go to the place whence thou camest!' Then, again, another preacher came, and began to teach us, and to say, 'You must not steal, nor lie, nor get drunk, and so forth.' We answered, 'Thou fool, dost thou think that we do not know that? Learn first thyself, and then teach the people to whom thou belongest to leave off these things. For who steal, or lie, or who are more drunken than thine own people?' And then we dismissed him. But Rauch came with a very different message.

> He told us of a Mighty One,
> The Lord of earth and sky,
> Who left His glory in the Heavens,
> For men to bleed and die;
> Who loved poor Indian sinners still,
> And longed to gain their love,
> And be their Saviour here
> And in His Father's house above.
> And when his tale was ended—

'My friends,' he gently said,
'I am weary with my journey,
And would fain lay down my head';
So beside our spears and arrows
He laid him down to rest,
And slept as sweetly as the babe
upon its mother's breast.

Then we looked upon each other,
And I whispered, 'This is new;
Yes, we have heard glad tidings,
And that sleeper knows them true;
He knows he has a Friend above,
Or would he slumber here,
With men of war around him,
And the war-whoop in his ear?
So we told him on the morrow
That he need not journey on,
But stay and tell us further
Of that loving, dying One;
And thus we heard of Jesus first,
And felt the wondrous power,
Which makes His people willing,
In His own accepted hour.

"Thus," added Tschoop, "through the grace of God an awakening took place among us. I say, therefore, Brethren, preach Christ our Savior, and His sufferings and death, if you will have your words to gain entrance among the heathen."[8]

In January, 1742, Rauch and Gottlob Buttner, a Moravian who had joined him at Shekomeko, were called to a synod at Oley, Pennsylvania. They were accompanied by three

[8] James Hutton, *History of the Moravian Church*, Second Edition, Moravian Publications Office, London, 1909., Book II, Capter 14.

of the Indian converts. The three Indians were baptized and became what Moravians described as the "first fruits" of the Moravian Mission in North America. At their baptisms they were given Christian names. Later that summer the first Moravian Christian Indian congregation was formed at Shekomeko with the assistance of Count Zinzendorf. At the end of 1743, the number of baptized Indians had increased to sixty-three. The efforts also led to establishment of two missions in nearby Connecticut.

The success of the missionaries caused alarm among white colonists in the area. The christianizing of the Indians hurt the business of traders who traded liquor to the Indians in exhange for furs and deer skins, so they were hostile. Also there was a war going on at the time with the French, and rumors were spread that the Moravians were Catholics and were influencing the Indians to side with the French. In fact the Moravians in accordance with their beliefs were teaching the Indians to avoid fighting for either side.

King George's War was primarily a European war which followed the death of a Hapsburg Emperor to determine who would succeed to the throne. England and France entered the war on opposite sides. At that time the British controlled the eastern seaboard from Georgia to Maine and the French controlled Canada and the lands west of the Appalachian Mountains. The New York authorities succeeded in enlisting the aid of the Iroquois to fight on the British side. This provoked the French to attack and burn Saratoga in retaliation. They also attacked Albany. The four year war was concluded in 1748 by the Treaty of Aux-La-Chapelle which restored the status quo in the colonies prior to its outbreak. In view of the effort of New York authorities to persuade the Indians to fight the French, it is understandable why they would not be pleased with the pacifist message of the Moravian missionaries.

Enemies of the Moravians ultimately succeeded in directing the attention of New York Governor George Clinton to the Shekomeko colony. The missionaries were ordered to appear before the Governor and his Council in New York in July 1744. Although acquitted of any wrong doing, they were cautioned to conduct themselves so as to arouse no further suspicions. The legal actions taken against the Moravian leaders had been based on laws against the Jesuits, and the hearing showed that there clearly was no legal basis for such a charge since the Moravians were a Protestant church which had been persecuted by Catholics for centuries. In order to provide a legal basis for attacking the Moravians, the Provincial Assembly, on September 22, 1744, adopted a law which said no "vagrant preacher, Moravian or disguised Papists, shall preach or teach either in public or private" without first swearing the oath and receiving a license. In accordance with their reading of the teachings of Scripture, the Moravians like the Quakers and Mennonites did not believe in taking oaths. On December 15, 1744, under orders from Governor Clinton, the sheriff and three peace justices of Dutchess County appeared at Shekomeko, and gave notice to the missionaries to cease their teachings. Rauch and Buttner and the other missionaries were summoned to appear in court at Poughkeepsie. Buttner was too ill to appear; but the others appeared and heard the new law read. There was no choice but to assure the court that the missionary effort at Shekomeko would end. Buttner died in February, 1745, and was buried at Shekomeko. Before he died he urged his Indian friends to remain faithful and not give up hope.

The New York authorities also arrested David Zeisberger and Frederick Post who were visiting the chief of the Mohawks to learn the Mohawk language. They were taken to New York where they spent fifty-one days in jail before their friends were able to secure their release. At the time of their arrest the officer told them, "If you or any of your

Brethren come here again without a pass from the Governor, I will have you whipped out of town."[9]

Even though the missionary effort in New York had to cease, the Moravians did not abandon their Mohican converts. Spangenberg led a party to the capital of the Iroquois at Onandaga, New York to secure permission to move the Mohicans to the Wyoming valley on the Susquehanna in Pennsylvania. The Iroquois Council renewed the treaty of friendship made with the Count and approved the relocation. When the news was delivered to the Mohicans at Shekomeko, they objected to the location. They pointed out that it was located on the warriors path which the Iroquois took on their way south to fight the Catawbas. The Mohicans feared that if they located a village there, they would be visited frequently by war parties causing disruption of village life. The Moravians then invited them to Bethlehem which they were happy to accept. Cabins were erected for them near Bethlehem, and they began the move in the Spring of 1746. A permanent location was purchased for them at the forks of the Mahoning Creek and the Lehigh River on the north side of the Blue Mountains. The land was cleared and construction begun so that they could begin moving to the new village by June, 1746. The new mission village was called Gnadenhutten. By 1750 the Moravians had four missions and one mission station. By 1755 Gnadenhutten had progressed spiritually and materially so that visitors marvelled at what the Moravians and their Christian converts were able to accomplish.

The Moravians organized converts into villages of "Christian Indians", as they were then called, under the guidance of Moravian missionaries who were referred to as their teachers and Indian converts who were referred to as helpers. The Christian Indian villages organized by the

---

[9] Earl P. Olmstead, *David Zeisberger, A Life Among the Indians*, Kent State University, 1997, p. 35.

Moravians were not simply religious congregations. They addressed the serious problems of Indians who through extensive contact with the colonists had lost much of their earlier vitality and moral virtue. Tribes that lived close to the colonies suffered hunger from loss of their hunting grounds. They became dependent on trade in furs and deerskins for trade goods made by whites. This led to extensive hunting and exhaustion of the stock of wildlife on which their livelihood depended. White traders frequently traded liquor for furs and skins resulting in extensive alcohol abuse. Illnesses contracted from whites had substantially reduced Indian populations, which among Indians meant that the Great Spirit was punishing them. Contact with European culture had undermined much of their traditional way of life and virtue. Conflict between the two cultures was slowly undermining their faith in their traditional religion, worldview, and self-esteem. Alcohol abuse and other self-destructive behavior had become a serious problem among these people. The missions' introduction of Christianity to members of the Delaware, Mohican and other tribes filled their lives with spiritual purpose and taught them how to live in self-supporting communities which were not dependent upon hunting and the fur trade for survival. In order to avoid the corrupting influence of whites as well as unconverted Indians, the communities were usually located just beyond the edge of the frontier. However, when hostilities erupted between the Colonists and Indians, the missions found themselves in the midst of a war zone. Each side suspected them of aiding the enemy. The challenge for the Moravians and their Christian Indians missions was how to survive in this hostile world.

CHAPTER 5

PREACHING LOVE IN A WORLD OF HATE AND VIOLENCE

The French and Indian War was sparked by a contest between the French and British for control of the rich fur trade in the Ohio valley. In order to establish their domination, the French constructed forts extending from Lake Erie south to what is now Pittsburgh where Fort Duquesne was constructed at the strategic forks of the Ohio River. The War began in 1754 when a party of Virginia militia under the leadership of George Washington who was on its way to Fort Duquesne fought with a French scouting party at Great Meadow. The British then sent General Braddock with a large British and Colonial force to capture Fort Duquesne. Braddock was defeated by a combined French and Indian force on July 9, 1755 near the Fort, and the tribes, sensing an opportunity to push the British colonies back, attacked the settlements all along the frontier. Entire communities along the frontier were massacred. Cabins were attacked and families killed or carried into captivity. Refugees from the attacks straggled into Bethlehem, Nazareth, and other Moravian towns seeking food, shelter and protection. Militia units marched in and out of the towns.

The mission at Gnadenhutten became a casualty of the war. The missionaries who served the mission lived together in a large mission house next to the chapel. On the evening of November 24, 1755, hearing the dogs barking outside, they opened the door to see who was there. They saw before them a war party of painted Indians who immediately opened fire killing several of the missionaries. Some escaped to the second story and closed and bolted the door. The Indians then set fire to the house. Except for two who jumped from the window and escaped to tell what happened, the missionaries who sought refuge in the second story died in the smoke and flames. The Christian Indians who lived across the river from the mission house fled to Bethlehem for protection.

In view of their pacifist principles, the Moravians had to decide what their policy would be. Would they abandon their pacifist principles completely and fight back, or would they not defend themselves if attacked? They decided on a middle ground. The towns were fortified and sentinels were posted around the towns so that hostile Indians would know that if they attacked, they would be discovered and the town would defend itself. The strategy was based on knowledge that Indians seldom attacked unless they could surprise their victims. The plan worked and the Moravian towns were never attacked.

The experience in North Carolina was similar to that in Pennsylvania. The War broke out soon after Bethabara was settled. Located on the frontier, the Moravian villages in North Carolina were surrounded by hostile Indian war parties and served as a refuge for settlers in the area. The villages were fortified and posted guards to show would-be attackers that they were vigilant. They also were never attacked.

The Moravians played an important role in treaty negotiations with the Delaware at Easton, Pennsylvania in 1756, 1757 and 1758. By the conclusion of the 1758 conference the Delaware had decided to withdraw from the conflict. The War finally ended with the French surrender of Quebec, Montreal and Detroit in 1760. A peace treaty was signed in 1763, whereby the French ceded their claims to Canada and the west to the British. The war had devastated the Moravian missionary program. In addition to the thriving mission at Gnadenhutten, the struggling mission at Shamokin in the Wyoming valley and the other missions had all been abandoned and destroyed. The Moravians continued to operate a mission at Nain close to Bethlehem which they had constructed after Gnadenhutten was destroyed to house the refugees from Gnadenhutten. In order to relieve overcrowding at Nain, in 1760 they constructed a new mission across the Blue Mountains from Bethlehem called Wechquetank.

Following the end of the War the Moravians in March 1762 sent veteran missionary Frederick Post and his young assistant John Heckewelder to the Muskingum valley in Ohio to invite the western Indians to a peace conference at Lancaster, Pennsylvania and to establish a mission among the western Delaware. They built their cabin near the Great Crossing (near present day Bolivar, Ohio), a junction on the Indian trail from Pittsburgh to Detroit and the trail from Lake Erie to the upper Shawnee villages on the Scioto River. Soon thereafter, Post returned to Lancaster, Pennsylvania with some of the leaders of the western Delaware for the treaty conference. Heckewelder was left alone in the wilderness while unknown to him the tribes of the Ohio country were preparing for war. After the British defeated the French, Lord Amherst, the British commander in America, treated the Indians with arrogance and contempt. Although the Treaty of Easton had promised that white expansion would stop at the mountains, settlers surged westward into the Ohio River Valley invading the Indians' hunting grounds. British traders, unlike the French, took advantage of the Indians. The western Indians became inflamed with hatred for the English, and under the leadership of Pontiac, a chief of the Ottawa tribe, united in an effort to drive them into the sea. Heckewelder barely escaped with his life.

With lightening speed the Indians captured most of the British forts west of the Alleghenies, and killed or captured all their defenders. Only the forts at Detroit, Pittsburgh and Niagara remained, and hostile Indians surrounded them. War parties once again attacked the cabins and settlements along the frontiers, and thousands of settlers were killed. Survivors fled eastward with tales of atrocities. The frontier folk, many of whom were Scotch-Irish, became inflamed with hatred of the Indians. Many believed that the "only good Indian was a dead Indian." Their feelings were aggravated by the failure of the government in Philadelphia, which was dominated by peace-loving Quakers, to take action to defend them. They felt that the Quakers cared more for the Indians than for them.

On August 20, 1763, a small group of Christian Indians that included a man, two women and a child were sleeping in a barn under the protection of a militia unit. Late at night the men, emboldened by drink, beat one of the women to death and then stabbed the man, his wife and their child to death. The whites in the area learning that the man had four brothers at the Moravian mission at Wechquetank concluded that the Indians there would retaliate. The militia approached the mission with the intent of attacking and destroying it. The missionary was able to convince them that they had nothing to fear from the converts. However, the militia unit that had committed the murders was subsequently attacked by a war party of hostile Delaware and many killed. A storm of fury swept the county and mobs gathered to attack the Christian Indian villages at Nain and Wechquetank. Fortunately a violent rainstorm quenched their ardor, and the missions were spared for the time being. The Moravians quickly moved the Indians residing at Wechquetank to Nazareth for their protection. Shortly after they left, the mission was burned down. Fearing that the Christian Indians in their charge would be massacred, the Moravians sent a delegation to Governor Penn, grandson of the colony's founder, seeking his protection. The Governor with the approval of his Council directed that the Indians be sent to Philadelphia where they were to be housed in the soldiers' barracks for their protection. However, when the wagons full of Christian Indians and Moravian missionaries arrived in Philadelphia on November 11, 1763, and despite the sympathy of the Quakers living there, they were surrounded by an angry mob demanding that they be killed. The British soldiers refused to allow the Indians in the barracks. After enduring the abuse of the mob for five hours, they were taken by boat to Province Island located south of town. It was the small pox quarantine area for the City. The Indians and missionaries were housed in two hospital buildings on the Island.

On December 14, 1763, a gang of Scotch-Irish vigilantes known as "The Paxton Boys" attacked a peaceful village of Conestoga Indians. The village contained the surviving remnant of a once great tribe that had lived peacefully with their white neighbors for sixty years. The six Indians found at the village were bludgeoned to death and the houses in the village were burned. The sheriff took the remaining fourteen residents of the village who were hunting at the time of the attack to the jail at Lancaster for their protection. The Paxton Boys rode into town heavily armed to finish the job that they had started at the Conestoga village. An eyewitness who arrived shortly after the gang had finished described the scene as follows:

> Oh what a horrid sight presented itself to my view!! - Near the back door of the prison lay an old Indian and his squaw particularly well-known and esteemed by the people of the town on account of his placid and friendly conduct... across him and his squaw lay two children of about the age of three years whose heads

were split with a tomahawk, and their scalps taken off. Towards the middle of the gaol yard, along the west side of the wall, lay a stout Indian I particularly noticed to have been shot in the breast, his legs were chopped with a tomahawk, his hands cut off, and finally a rifle discharged in his mouth so that his head was blown to atoms, and the brains were splashed against and yet hanging to the wall for three or four feet around. The man's hands and feet had also been chopped off with a tomahawk. In this manner lay the whole of them, men, women and children, spread about the prison yard: shot, scalped, - hacked and cut to pieces.[10]

News of the massacre caused outrage and alarm in Philadelphia. The Governor issued proclamations for the arrest and conviction of the murderers. Despite the offer of an award of 200 pounds, no arrests were ever made. Rumors flew that the Paxton Boys were on their way to Philadelphia to murder the Indians who had been sheltered there. The Moravians sent a delegation from Bethlehem to Philadelphia to protect them. The Governor decided to send them to New York. They were loaded on boats and began their journey only to learn that New York would not accept them. They were returned to Philadelphia and housed in the barracks. The Governor then learned that a force of 1500 from the frontier counties was marching toward Philadelphia to demand that the Christian Indians be turned over to them. The Governor aided by Benjamin Franklin rallied the people to defend the town, and six hundred volunteered to come to its defense. When the insurgents appeared, they learned that the town was prepared to defend itself. Franklin was able to persuade them to return

---

[10] Paul A. Wallace, *Thirty Thousand Miles with John Heckewelder*, Pittsburgh: University of Pittsburgh Press, 1958 p. 77.

home based on a promise that their concerns about protection of the frontier would be addressed.

The resistance of the Indians came to an end when Col. Henry Bouquet led a large army west to relieve the siege of Fort Pitt, and then in October, 1764, led an army of 1500 British and American Colonial troops to the Muskingum River in Ohio near present day Coshocton, Ohio. Unable to confront such a large force, the Ohio Indians were completely subdued and turned over their white captives.

Although the Christian Indians sheltered in Philadelphia escaped murder, many of them did not escape death. While housed at the barracks, 42 of the 125 converts died of small pox. By February 1765, hostility had subsided so that the survivors could leave Philadelphia. Throughout the ordeal the Moravians had remained beside their Christian Indian brethren and endured the hatred, abuse and threats of irate whites. They had cared for the sick and dying. They learned that despite the assistance of the Governor and Quakers in Philadelphia, it meant nothing to most of the frontier people that these Indians were devoted Christians. The Moravians learned the bitter lesson that in order to survive their missions must be located away from white settlements.

Upon their return from Philadelphia the Moravians took the Christian Indians deep into country controlled by the Iroquois. With the blessing of the Iroquois, a mission was established on the Susquehanna named Friedenshutten or "Huts of Peace". In six years the mission grew to 150 inhabitants. The residents were housed in 29 well-built log houses with glass windows, doors and chimneys similar to the homes of white settlers and 13 Indian style bark huts. Houses were located on both sides of a single street. The chapel was located in the center of the street, flanked by a schoolhouse. Opposite the chapel was the mission house where the missionaries stayed. Behind the houses were individual gardens and orchards. The town was surrounded by a post and rail fence. The street was kept scrupulously clean. Between the village and the river were more than 250 acres of well-tilled farmland and pasture surrounded by fences. The villagers had a large collection of cattle, hogs, and chickens. A fleet of canoes was moored at the river. In quality of life Friedenshutten was the equal to any white settlement of similar size. Once again the progress made with this village showed what the Moravians were able to accomplish when allowed to work with the Indians free of interference from hostile whites and Indians.

In 1767 the Moravians received an invitation from an Indian village on the Allegheny River in western Pennsylvania. They sent a party of missionaries and converts to visit them. The village was comprised of former members of various tribes dislocated as a result of western migration in response to white settlement. It was under the protection of the Seneca, a tribe of the Iroquois federation, who controlled the region. The trip led to the establishment of a mission on the Allegheny despite the opposition of the Indian's religious leader there. The battle for the souls of the villagers was waged between their traditional religious leader who preached that the God of the Indians was a different God and their path to Heaven a different path than the God and path to Heaven of the white man and the missionaries. The missionaries won a number of converts among these people. However, in view of continuing opposition, the missionaries decided to accept an invitation to move further westward to the Beaver River west of Pittsburgh. Before leaving Zeisberger left the Indians on the Allegheny with the following message which set forth the Moravians' view of the world and their mission in it:

> I have on several occasions told you we are a people different from others ... We (Christian Indians) are not able to live as other Indians do, we do not like heathenism, on the contrary we abhor it. We live only

to please the Savior and to do his work. It is the same with us white brethren (missionaries). We are separate from the world. There are only two kinds of people in all the nations of the world; namely, children of the world and children of the Savior; the former are on the way to eternal destruction, the latter on the way to eternal life. I have often heard that many of you have said: Why should we believe in the white people, they look quite different than we do, because their skin is white and ours is brown. We do not want you to believe in the white people but in the Savior, because you can learn very bad things from the white people, things that are even worse than you do. You call me Schwannak, which means white man; we can see that you do not make any difference between us and all other white people. Try and use your intelligence and judgment which God has given you and open your eyes, then you will see the difference! I take it you realize that my way of living is different from that of other white people. We are children of God and all those who believe in God and his five wounds are our brothers and sisters whether their skin is white, brown or black ... All together we form one people of God.[11]

The Moravian message sounds very modern in its call for racial equality. At the time this was a radical idea that challenged the beliefs of most whites and Indians. The religious message may sound intolerant and strident to many modern ears. However, it was made by people who had absolutely no doubt that belief in Christ was the only salvation for all people of the world. They were driven by their

---

[11] Tilda Marx, trans., *Diaries of the Moravian Missionaries in Western Pennsylvania, 1769-1772.* Unpublished manuscript commissioned by Merle Deardorff, Warren Historical Society, Warren, Pennsylvania, pp. 90-91.

compassion for people who knew nothing of Christ and faced eternal damnation unless the message was brought to them, and they chose to be saved. Despite romantic notions that we may have about Indian culture from the distant perspective of the 21st century, they were quite aware of the cruelty, alcohol abuse, indolence, thievery, and deviousness that characterized that culture after extensive contact with white culture. They were able to convince many Indians to believe in Jesus as their Savior, despite the fact that He lived in a land half way around the world from them and lived in a culture totally different from their own. In so doing these Indians abandoned the view of the world and the religion which they had been taught since childhood, the religion which for generations had provided satisfactory answers to their people for the big questions for which humans in all places and at all times have sought answers. Their decision was no less remarkable than the decision of the ancestors of the English, Irish, Scot, and German colonists of Pennsylvania who abandoned their traditional religion to embrace Christianity centuries earlier. Each baptism was a thrill not only for each Indian who experienced it, but also for the missionaries who witnessed it.

In 1770 the Moravians moved their mission on the Allegheny to a new mission on the Beaver River west of Pittsburgh. This time they established their village near a village of Delaware and Munsee. Here again they won new converts. David McClure, a Presbyterian minister, visited the village in 1772 and described the village as follows:

> It was a neat Moravian village consisting of one street and houses pretty compact, on each side, with gardens in the back. There was a convenient log church with a small bell in which the Indians assembled for the morning and evening prayer.

After staying at the village for several days, McClure made the following observations:

> The Moravians appear to have adopted the best mode of Christianizing the Indians. They go among them without noise and parade and by their friendly behavior conciliate their good will. They join them in the chase and freely distribute to the helpless and gradually instill into the minds of individuals, the principles of religions. They then invite those who are disposed to harken to them, to retire to some convenient place at a distance from the wild Indians, and assist them to build a village, and teach them to plant and sow, and carry on some course manufactures. Those Indians, thus separated, reverence and love their instructors, as their fathers, and withdraw a connection with the wild Indians.[12]

The proximity of the mission on Beaver Creek to the Indian village created problems because of frequent drunkenness of the unconverted Indian villagers. Certainly one of the worse curses brought by whites to the Indians was liquor. Unscrupulous traders, knowing the Indians' low resistance, would ply them with liquor and then exchange liquor for furs and skins. Then all of the men, women and children of the Indian's village would go on drinking binges that would last until the liquor was consumed. Drunkenness frequently led to fights and murder and then another murder in retaliation. It also led to hunger and even starvation as energy and resources were diverted from productive activity to drinking. In many tribes the members were divided between drinking Indians who adhered to the old beliefs and practices

---

[12] *Diary of David McClure, 1748-1820*, New York: The Knickerbocker Press, 1899. pp. 50-51.

and "praying Indians" who converted to Christianity and did not drink. Although drinking was prohibited in all the Moravian missions, access to alcohol through nearby white traders or Indian villages where drinking took place was considered a temptation and threat to the Christian Indians at the mission. The proximity to a tribe of drinking Indians made the mission's location on the Beaver undesirable.

David McClure, the Presbyterian missionary, who visited the Indians on the Muskingum River in Ohio in 1772, witnessed a drunken frolic at one of the Indian villages where he was invited to stay. He described what he saw as follows:

> By midnight the body of the inhabitants of both sexes were drunk... The ground trembled with the tramping of feet; hooping, yells, singing, laughter, and the voice of rage and madness were blended in dreadful discord, adding horror to the darkness of midnight.... This horrid scene gave some idea of the infernal regions, where sin and misery hold a universal sway. I rose with the appearance of light, and with an Indian trader, whom I met at the door, walked through the village. The noise and uproar continued. In one place sat several on the ground drinking rum from wooden bowls – others lay stretched out in profound sleep – some were reeling and tumbling over the green, and one or two companies were fighting, and yelling in the most frightful manner.... It was a horrid spectacle.... In our walk a fierce Indian mad with rage came up and shaking his fist at me used high and threatening words.... I was a little alarmed at his threatening gestures and wrathful voice and looks as well as the angry looks of some others of the warriors. The men and women this morning were naked except a piece of blue cloth, about their loins, to cover their shame. It is

the nature of this shameless vice to obliterate all sense of modesty.[13]

Lest one think drinking was only a problem in Indian villages, McClure on the same journey described Pittsburgh as follows, "Drinking, debauchery and all kinds of vice reign in this frontier of depravity."[14]

The Moravians were looking for a new location for the 124 converts living at the Beaver mission who were Delaware and Munsee. They also needed a new location for the Delaware at Friedenshutten on the Susquehanna because the Iroquois had recently sold the land where the village was located to the proprietors of Pennsylvania. White settlers would soon be locating near them. There was also a mission of fifty Mohican that faced a similar problem. The Council of the Delaware located on the Muskingum River in Ohio sent an invitation to relocate the Christian Indians there. The capital of the Delaware was located at the forks of the Muskingum, Tuscarawas, and Walhonding at present day Coshocton. Originally located in eastern Pennsylvania, the Delaware had moved westward because of the French and Indian and Pontiac's Wars and because of white expansion. The Wyandotte had granted them permission to settle in eastern Ohio. The Council expressed a desire to relocate the Christian Delaware who lived in the missions in Pennsylvania to the new Delaware homeland where they would be closer to friends and relatives and under the protection of the tribe. It also expressed a desire to have the missionaries bring their message to the Delaware on the Muskingum.

In May 1772 the Moravians began construction of their new mission located on the Muskingum River in Ohio (now

---

[13]   *The Diary of David McClure*, New York: The Knickerbocker Press, 1899., pp. 73-75.

[14]   *The Diary of David McClure*, New York: The Knickerbocker Press, 1899, p. 109.

known as the Tuscarawas River) about 20 miles from the tribal capital of the Delaware. They called their new village Schoenbrunn that is German for beautiful spring.[15] The residents of the Pennsylvania missions were moved to the new mission on the Muskingum. When the Mohican arrived, a second village was begun at a location eight miles from Schoenbrunn. It was named Gnadenhutten in remembrance of the mission in Pennsylvania where the massacre had occurred in 1755. By the end of 1773 there were 184 residents at Schoenbrunn and 108 at Gnadenhutten. The mission program seemed to be a resounding success, and the Moravians were filled with optimism. The missions were located northwest of the Ohio River where under existing treaties white settlement was prohibited. They were under the protection of the Delaware that were supportive of the missions. The Delaware had peaceful relations with the whites at Pittsburgh and the other western tribes. However, passions of hate and anger were about to surround the peaceful little missions on the Muskingum with hostility and once again test the Moravians and their converts.

In 1774 controversy erupted in western Pennsylvania when Virginians under the leadership of Dr. John Connolly forcefully seized control of Pittsburgh and western Pennsylvania in the name of their colony. For a time both Pennsylvania and Virginia claimed jurisdiction over the area. Both colonies had county officials attempting to govern the same territory. This created uncertainty for the Moravians because they had a long-standing relationship with the Pennsylvania government.

In 1768 the Treaty of Fort Stanwix was signed with the Iroquois that extended the boundary of white settlement from the headwaters of the Alleghenies to the Ohio River and

---

[15] The reconstructed village is a state memorial operated by the Ohio Historical Society and is located within the City of New Philadelphia, Ohio.

opened Kentucky to white settlement. White settlers began to pour into Kentucky. This caused great consternation among the Shawnee who considered Kentucky to be their hunting grounds. The Shawnee had not been a party to the treaty and did not recognize the authority of the Iroquois, who were centered in New York, to give away their hunting grounds in Kentucky. Connolly, in a deliberate attempt to provoke an incident that would spark a war, informed the leaders of the small white settlement at Wheeling to prepare for an imminent attack by the Shawnee. The backwoodsmen along the eastern bank of the Ohio considered it a declaration of War, and began attacking Indians   in the vicinity. A Mingo village under the leadership of Chief Logan was located on the west bank of the Ohio north of Wheeling and south of present day Steubenville. Logan had always maintained friendly relations with the whites. He had been named for the man who had served as William Penn's deputy for years. The Indians from the Mingo village frequently crossed the river to buy liquor and other supplies from their white neighbors, the Bakers. On April 30, 1774, when Logan was absent from camp, two men and two women crossed the river from the Mingo Village with a baby and were invited to engage in a shooting match. After they discharged their guns, the men and women were murdered. Later in the day, other Mingo crossed the river to check on the first group and met the same fate. A total of twelve Mingo were killed including all of Logan's relatives. News of the massacre set off shock waves along the frontier as whites prepared for the inevitable retaliation. Chief Logan dedicated himself to exacting revenge.

The Christian Indians assisted Captain White Eyes, a Delaware chieftain, in maintaining the peace among the Delaware and in negotiating with the Shawnee to avoid a war. However, Governor Dunmore of Virginia prompted by Connolly ordered Virginia Militia to march for the Ohio to attack the Shawnee. One of the militia forces attacked and burned Shawnee and Mingo villages on the Muskingum south of the Delaware villages, but due to the efforts of Captain White Eyes and others, spared the Delaware who remained neutral in the conflict. The Shawnee attacked the militia army camped at Point Pleasant on the south side of the Ohio near the mouth of the Great Kanawha. After a fierce daylong battle, the Shawnee withdrew, and Cornstalk, the Shawnee chief sued for peace. Dunmore led his army into the Scioto Valley and with the assistance of Captain White Eyes negotiated a peace treaty with Cornstalk that spared the Shawnee villages. Notwithstanding the Treaty, Dunmore had to threaten the leader of the militia that had been attacked at Point Pleasant to prevent him from destroying the villages. The Shawnee agreed to surrender their claim to Kentucky and not attack whites on the Ohio River. The northwest side of the Ohio was to remain free of white settlement. Since the Mingo refused to negotiate, a force was sent to destroy their villages on the Scioto. Chief Logan, who refused to participate in the treaty negotiations, sent the following message to Governor Dunmore:

> I appeal to any white man to say if he ever entered Logan's cabin hungry and I gave him not meat; if he ever came cold or naked and I gave him not clothing. During the course of the last long and bloody war, Logan remained idle in his tent, an advocate for peace. Nay, such was my love for the whites that those of my own country pointed to me as I passed and said, "Logan is the friend of the white man." I had even thought to have lived with you, but for the injuries of one man. Colonel Cresap, the last spring in cold blood and unprovoked, murdered all the relatives of Logan, not sparing even my women and children. There runs not a drop of my blood in the veins of any living creature. This called on me for revenge. I have sought it. I have killed many. I have fully glutted my

vengeance. For my country I rejoice at the beams of peace; but do not harbor the thought that mine is the joy of fear. Logan never felt fear. He will not turn on his heel to save his life. Who is there to mourn for Logan? Not one.[16]

Lord Dunmore's War was over, but the conflict aroused animosity among many of the Delaware toward the Christian Indians and their missionaries. It also revealed that the invitation to the Moravians had been a ruse by Chief Netawatwes and his Council to persuade them to bring the Christian Delaware to the Delaware capital to augment its population. Once the Christian Indians were settled on the Muskingum, the Council planned to demand that the missionaries leave or be killed. Captain White Eyes discovered the plan and confronted the Chief and Council with their deception. The Chief, regretting his participation in the strategy, reversed himself and encouraged the Moravians to establish a new Mission close to the Delaware capital located at present day Coshocton, Ohio. The purpose of the mission was to make it easier for residents of the Delaware village to attend services and become better acquainted with the Moravians' teaching. The Moravians began construction of the new mission in April 1776. They called it Lichtenau, which in English means "Pasture of Light." By the end of the year there were over 400 Christian Indians living at the three missions of Schoenbrunn, Gnadenhutten, and Lichtenau.

The Revolutionary War was a difficult time for the Moravians. They did not as a matter of conscience believe in taking oaths or bearing arms. When the War began, the Moravians did not share the hostility of many of the other colonials toward the British government because of the

---

[16] John S.C. Abbott, *The History of the State of Ohio*, Detroit: Northwestern Publishing Company, 1875, p. 161. Logan was wrong in his accusation of Cresap. It was Greathouse who planned and led the attack.

assistance that they had received in establishing their American missions. The British parliament had formally recognized their church and granted them immunity from military service. Prominent Englishmen had assisted in establishing the first mission in Georgia and the mission in North Carolina. Furthermore, their religious teaching taught them to submit to those in authority, and it was not at all clear that the Revolution would succeed.

The Quakers, Mennonites, and other small religious sects in Pennsylvania also faced problems of conscience as a result of their beliefs. Unlike the Quakers and the Mennonites, who also did not believe in oaths and military service, the Moravians believed signing of oaths and participation in the War was a matter of individual conscience. The Moravians did not punish members who chose to serve. On June 2, 1775, Benjamin Franklin, then a member of the Continental Congress, wrote to Moravian Bishop Seidel assuring him that he would exert his influence to prevent any molestation of the Moravians because of their religious principles. However, he reminded the Bishop of the defensive posture which they had taken during the French and Indian War and suggested that it might be prudent to allow any of their young men who were willing to learn how to use arms for defensive purposes only.[17] Knowing what the Moravians had gone through during the French and Indian War and Pontiac's War, Franklin's suggestion was intended as a measure, which the Moravians could take to help diffuse and deter neighborhood hostility.

The Moravians sought to have the oath changed to accommodate their beliefs, and they tried to reach agreement for alternatives to military service or payment in lieu of such service. Although Congress took no action, the Pennsylvania Assembly passed a series of resolves to permit pacifists to

---

[17] *Letters of Delegates to Congress 1774-1789*, Vol. 1, Washington: Library of Congress, 1976, pp. 433-434.

make contributions in lieu of bearing arms. When summoned to appear before the Governor and Council of New Jersey, the Brethren appeared and submitted the following:

> We do not believe that you can question that we are good and peaceable inhabitants of the country, friends of all men and dangerous to none. We hope, therefore, that you will not constrain us to take the oath renouncing allegiance and the oath of loyalty, because it is contrary to our religious principles to take said oaths. We shall endeavor to lead a quiet and peaceable life in all godliness and honesty, as we have done hitherto; nor shall we undertake anything that would be disadvantageous or harmful to the government under which we live and enjoy the blessing of conscience, for freedom of conscience is more precious to us than life itself.[18]

Count Zinzendorf several years before the American Revolution had admonished the Brethren as follows:

> Our Savior has said wars are no concern of ours; nations shall rise against nation, but we are to remain quiet and attend to our work. If we concern ourselves with soldiery at all, it must simply be because they need our help as human beings; in that case we shall not fail in performing our humanitarian and Christian duty.

Those who felt that anyone who did not share their zeal for the war was a traitor subjected the Moravians to accusations of disloyalty, threats, and persecution. Fines were exacted;

---

[18] Kenneth Gardiner Hamilton, *John Ettwein and the Moravian Church during the Revolutionary Period*, quoting a manuscript prepared by John Ettwein on the Revolution, p. 171.

livestock and grain seized for the war effort; imprisonment threatened; vicious slanders circulated; and insults, ridicule and abuse heaped upon them.

Nonetheless, for the most part the Moravians in Pennsylvania escaped serious persecution because they did render valuable service to the Revolutionary cause. In 1776 the British defeated the Americans on Long Island and took possession of New York City. Washington's army retreated into Pennsylvania pursued by the British. Because of the retreat of the army, the hospital had to be relocated. General George Washington ordered that the General Hospital for the army be moved to Bethlehem. The sick and wounded arrived in December and the Moravians made room for them, fed them, comforted them, and that winter buried 110 of them. During the War buildings at the Moravian communities of Bethlehem, Nazareth, and Lititz were used as hospitals. Wagonloads of injured soldiers arrived at the villages to discharge their maimed and dying cargo. The Moravians spent countless hours caring for and comforting the wounded and sick soldiers and providing spiritual support. Some of those tending the sick contracted their diseases and died. Many of the soldiers died and were buried at the villages. Those who survived, including officers like Lafayette, remembered the compassionate treatment received from the Moravians.

The Revolution's impact on the Moravians in the South was quite different from the Moravians in Pennsylvania. Following the French and Indian War and Pontiac's War the western frontier of North Carolina became embroiled in the "Regulator" movement. Many of the Scotch-Irish settlers in the west were hostile to taxes and the colonial government that sought to impose them. At one point the Regulators took over a courthouse, deposing the county judge and local assemblyman. The Moravians would have nothing to do with the movement, and therefore were a target of Regulator hostility. The movement was crushed when their "army" was defeated by the Governors troops at the Battle of Almance Creek in 1771. When the Revolutionary War began many of the Scotch-Irish neighbors of the Moravians harbored resentments from the Regulator period. In western North Carolina, the Revolution produced an acrimonious civil war, with attachments to each side based more on family ties and personal loyalty to leaders than to differences in values or background. Toward the end of the War, when the British focused their military effort on the south, British and Colonial troops passed through Wachovia. This heightened the stress on the Moravians because each side demanded supplies and accused the Moravians of aiding the enemy. There were several times when they feared their towns would be burned. The Moravians simply wanted to be left alone. Although there were close calls and frequent extortions and pillaging, the communities did survive the War.

Like in the north, the first issues that the North Carolina Moravians faced were over loyalty oaths and enrollment in the militia. Although many Moravians refused to sign the oath or to join the militia, like their Brethren in the north, the Moravians left the matter up to individual conscience and did not expel members who signed the oath or joined the militia. The Moravians petitioned the State's Revolutionary assembly for exemption, which was at first denied. In 1779 the Assembly reversed itself and allowed the Moravians to sign a modified oath that they had proposed and granted them exemption from military duty if they paid a three-fold tax.

Even though the Moravians reached an accommodation with the State's Revolutionary leaders, this did not protect them from local militia and marauding gangs of thugs who periodically descended on the villages threatening to burn them to the ground, demanding their goods, horses, cattle, and grain, and occasionally beating up on Moravians. Many of the Scotch-Irish settlers who lived on the western frontier had never cared for the Moravians. The Moravians spoke German; they practiced a strange religion; because of their discipline and organization, they appeared affluent compared to many of their Scotch-Irish neighbors; they sought to befriend and mission to the Indians whom the Scotch-Irish hated; they did not hate the British whom the Scotch-Irish hated; and they were pacifists which meant they would not bear arms against the British. Pacifism was a concept that was totally foreign to Scotch-Irish culture. Most importantly, they were defenseless. All of these factors made them targets for hostile neighbors. On the other hand, the Moravians were kind, gentle people, who were always fair in their dealings with others, and ready to give generously to avoid violence. They were blessed with leadership who were skilled in avoiding and dispelling confrontation. They were part of a church whose history was filled with long and bitter persecution, and their faith taught them that when they suffered, they were following in the footsteps of the Savior and his apostles who had also suffered and died.

The Moravian missionaries in the West were to face the greatest challenge from the Revolution. After the Revolutionary War erupted, British Governor Hamilton at Detroit was instructed to enlist the Ohio Indians on the British side, and encourage them to attack the Western frontiers. The strategy was intended to encourage the residents of the frontier counties to choose the British side or exert pressure on the easterners to end the War. It also was intended to accomplish the military objective of forcing the Colonies to commit resources to defending the frontier. The new Colonial Indian agent at Pittsburgh, James Morgan, attempted to counter the British strategy by encouraging the Ohio tribes to stay neutral in the conflict. The Americans sought not only to protect the frontiers from Indian attack but also to enable frontier militia to join the Colonial forces in the east. The Moravian missionaries and the Christian Indians assisted Morgan. A conference was held at Pittsburgh in October 1776, and was attended by Delaware, Shawnee and Seneca as well as leaders of the Christian Indians. The participants pledged to remain neutral, and the Americans pledged to respect the Ohio River as the existing boundary of white settlement as established by the 1768 Treaty. The Wyandotte who lived on the Sandusky River in north central Ohio declined to participate in the conference because they had not decided whether or not to join the British. The Mingo, still inflamed by the massacre of the residents of Logan's village and the destruction of their villages by Lord Dunmore's army, were already sending war parties to attack settlers on the Pennsylvania and Virginia frontiers.

Early in 1777 tensions began to mount within the mission as some of the Munsee joined the Mingo. Rumors were spread that a Mingo war party was on its way to kill the white missionaries. The Council of the Delaware at Coshocton encouraged the Moravians to abandon Schoenbrunn and Gnadenhutten, consolidate the missions at Lichtenau where the Delaware would be able to protect them, and send the missionaries who had families back east. In April 1777, Schoenbrunn was abandoned, the chapel burned to prevent its desecration, and the residents moved to Lichtenau and Gnadenhutten. Despite instructions to the contrary from the Delaware Council, Mingo war parties regularly passed through the two villages, announcing their arrival with the blood chilling "death-holler." On their trips back from the frontier, frightened captive while children would accompany them. The bloody scalps of the children's fathers and mothers would be hanging from the warriors' belts. All but two of the missionaries returned to Bethlehem.

By July of 1777 the Wyandotte had decided to join the British-inspired offensive against the frontier. They requested the Delaware to join them, but the Delaware insisted they were bound by treaty to remain neutral. David Zeisberger warned

General Hand, who was the new American commander at Pittsburgh, that unless an American army was sent out soon to the Ohio country, he feared that all the Ohio Indians would join with the British. A large Wyandotte war party stopped at Coshocton on its way to attack Fort Henry at Wheeling, and it seemed likely that the white missionaries would be killed. A leader of the Christian Indians pleaded with the Wyandotte chief to allow them to simply live peacefully with their white teachers who they looked upon as their own flesh and blood. The appeal saved the missionaries lives, and the Wyandotte chief had a friendly meeting with them.

In November 1777 Cornstalk, chief of the Shawnee, who had used his influence to keep the Shawnee from entering the War, and his son and two companions had gone for a friendly visit to Fort Randolph at Point Pleasant at the fork of the Ohio and Kanawha Rivers. The fort's commander thought he could assure good behavior of the Shawnee by seizing the chief and his party and holding them hostage. They were placed in a cabin at the fort. A few weeks later, a militiaman was slain by Indians outside the fort. An enraged mob entered the fort, broke into the cabin and murdered Cornstalk and his son. This senseless killing removed the last influential voice of restraint among the Shawnee.

In March 1778 Alexander McKee, Matthew Elliott, and Simon Girty defected to the British. McKee had served as the Indian agent for the British at Pittsburgh and would become the British Indian agent at Detroit. He and Elliott were Indian traders at Pittsburgh. Girty, captured as a boy and raised by Indians, had served as a scout and interpreter for the British. All three had many friends and considerable influence among the Ohio Indians. Their first stop after their flight from Pittsburgh was the Delaware capital on the Muskingum to persuade the Delaware to break their neutrality and join the War on the British side. They claimed that American armies in the east had been badly defeated, General Washington killed, members of Congress captured, and that an army of enraged easterners was on its way to attack Indians in the west. The Delaware Council was torn with uncertainty and teetered toward joining what appeared to be the winning side. Fortunately, the missionary John Heckewelder returned from the east while the meeting was going on with news that British General Burgoyne's army had been defeated at Saratoga. He brought letters from Morgan at Pittsburgh reassuring the Delaware of friendship, thanking them for their steadfast friendship and expressing optimism that in view of Burgoyne's defeat the War would soon be over. The lies of the McKee party were exposed, and the Delaware remained committed to neutrality.

In April of 1778 Gnadenhutten was abandoned. Its residents moved to Lichtenau so that all the Christian Indians were consolidated into one village close to the protection of the Delaware capital. By this time the Moravians feared not only the war parties of hostile Indians but also the risk of an attack by frontier militia who considered all Indians to be enemies.

Later in the year Zeisberger received a letter from Governor Hamilton at Detroit warning him to stop sending letters to Pittsburgh revealing plans of the British and their Indian allies. The Governor also sent a letter to the Delaware demanding that they join the British or be crushed. The Delaware then attended a conference at Pittsburgh where they were asked to sign a Treaty pledging their assistance to an offensive against the British and their Indian allies and consent to construction of an American fort in their territory. The treaty was the work of General Lachlan McIntosh, the new commander at Pittsburgh, and was negotiated without the involvement of George Morgan, the Indian agent, who was in the east at the time. It represented a reversal of the American policy of neutrality. The Delaware were deceived into signing it. After learning what happened, Morgan, said, "There never was a conference with the Indians so improperly or villainously conducted." Their trust in the Americans was betrayed. If they took an active role in the conflict on the side of the Americans, they placed themselves at risk of anhilation by the British and their Ohio Indian allies. Shortly thereafter White Eyes, the Delaware chief, who was appointed as scout for McIntosh's army and who had been primarily responsible for keeping the Delaware neutral was murdered by whites. The Delaware were told he died of small pox. He had been one of the most important friends of the Americans and Moravian missionaries among the Delaware. His death was followed by the arrival of McIntosh's army on the Tuscarawas River and the construction of Fort Laurens at the crossing of the Great Trail near present day Bolivar.[19] The sight of his rag tag army, short of supplies, did not inspire confidence among the Delaware that they were now safe from the British and their allies. His address to the assembled friendly Indians was arrogant and insulting and threatened them if they did not join the offensive against Detroit. Two hundred men were left at Fort Laurens to brave the winter with few supplies. The supply line was a long and difficult trail through the wilderness to Fort McIntosh on the Ohio River west of Pittsburgh. Hostile Indians attacked Fort Laurens and several Americans were killed. It was then besieged for an extended period, and the remaining men barely escaped starvation. The fort was finally relieved and then abandoned.

The change in American policy toward the Delaware requesting them to be active participants rather than neutral, the death of White Eyes, the demonstration of the weakness of American forces, the ineptitude of McIntosh, and the resignation of George Morgan as Indian Agent at Pittsburgh combined to undermine the Delaware's commitment to

---

[19] The site of Fort Laurens is a state memorial operated by the Ohio Historical Society near Bolivar, Ohio.

neutrality. Despite the efforts of the Christian Indians many in the tribe under the leadership of Captain Pipe now favored joining the alliance with the British and moved to the Sandusky River in northwestern Ohio near the Wyandotte. The Moravians, aware of the change in sentiment, no longer felt secure at Lichtenau because of its proximity to the Delaware capital. Gnadenhutten was reoccupied, and New Schoenbrunn was constructed across the river from the site of the old Schoenbrunn. At the request of the Delaware chiefs some of the Christian Indians remained at Lichtenau. As a result of increasing hostility, these Indians were moved in March 1780 to a new village located five miles from Gnadenhutten. The new village was called Salem which means peace. By the end of 1780 nearly four hundred converts lived at the three missions. An expanded staff of missionaries served them. They had little contact with the remaining Delaware, and war parties no longer stopped at the missions. They had completed their best year since 1775 and the future seemed promising.

In April 1781, after learning from the Moravians that the remaining Delaware at Coshocton were hostile and planning to join in the attacks on white settlements, the commander at Pittsburgh led an army to attack what was left of the Delaware capital. There was a spirited battle, and fifteen warriors were killed. Women and children were captured and then released. The Indian village and the abandoned buildings at Lichtenau were burned. This marked the end of Indian settlements on the Muskingum except for the Christian Indians living at the three missions. Colonel Brodhead met with the Moravian leaders and proposed that the missions be moved closer to Pittsburgh for protection. The Moravians and their converts decided to remain at their villages.

In August 1781, British Captain Matthew Elliot and the Wyandotte chiefs appeared at the villages with an army of three hundred Indians for the purpose of removing the

Christian Indians and the missionaries to the Sandusky River near the Wyandotte. The justification given for the action was an accusation that the Moravians had been sending letters to the commander at Pittsburgh warning them of Indian war parties. The missionaries attempted to persuade Elliot and the Wyandotte chief to postpone the move until the spring so that the Christian Indians could harvest their crops. From August 10 to September 3 the negotiations continued with neither side relenting. Finally, the Wyandotte patience ran out and the missionaries were seized by warriors, stripped, and confined with other prisoners for three days. The mission buildings were looted. The hogs and chickens killed. Recognizing that there was no choice, the missionaries agreed to assist with the move. The Christian Indians began their long trip down the Tuscarawas River to the site of the old Delaware capital, then up the Walhonding and Kokosing Rivers and then through the woods and swamps to the Sandusky River, near the Wyandotte capital close to present day Upper Sandusky, Ohio. They immediately went to work creating a new village at what came to be called Captive Town. The food that they brought with them was soon consumed, and so began their frantic efforts to find food for the party of more than three hundred Indians and missionaries.

Soon after they arrived, Zeisberger was summoned by Indian Agent McKee to appear before the British commander in Detroit. He left for Detroit with three other missionaries and three leaders of the Christian Indians. When he arrived, he learned that he was charged with treason for passing letters to the American commander at Pittsburgh. At his trial Captain Pipe, a Delaware Chief, who along with the Wyandotte Chief Half King had made the accusations against Zeisberger, was asked to speak. He said:

> Thou has ordered us to bring the believing Indians with their teachers from the Muskingum. We have done so,

and it has been done, as ordered us ... They are now here before thine eyes, thou canst now speak with them as thy desired, but thou wilt speak good words to them, and I say to thee, speak kindly to them, for they are our friends, and I hold them dear and should not like to see harm befall them.[20]

The perplexed commander demanded to know whether it was true that the missionaries had been corresponding with the rebels. The Chief acknowledged that "there might be some truth to the thing, and I cannot say it was all lies, but it will not happen again since they are away from there but now here."[21]

The Governor then asked what he should do with the missionaries. The Chief said he had promised the Christian Indians that their teachers could stay with them. After questioning Zeisberger further, the Commander dismissed the charge of treason. Before the missionaries left for the new village on the Sandusky, he complimented them on their work with the Indians and pledged his support. He also provided them generously with food and clothing. They were back at the village by the end of November.

The villagers spent the next few months struggling to avoid starvation. Zeisberger's wife Susan wrote, "Many times the Indians shared their last morsel with me, for many times I spend eight days in succession without any food of my own."[22] Zeisberger, always worrying foremost about the suffering of others, wrote "The hunger among our people here at home is so great that for some time already they have had to

---

[20] *Diary of David Zeisberger, A Moravian Missionary Among the Indians of Ohio*, translated and edited by Eugene F. Bliss, 2 vols., Cincinnati: R. Clarke, 1885, Vol 1, pp. 37-43.

[21] *Diary of David Zeisberger, A Moravian Missionary Among the Indians of Ohio*, translated and edited by Eugene F. Bliss, 2 vols., Cincinnati: R. Clarke, 1885, Vol 1, pp. 37-43.

[22] Susan Zeisberger's Memoir, Moravian Church Archives, Bethlehem, Pa.

live upon dead cattle, cows, and horses; never in their lives have they felt such want ... Why does the Savior let all this come upon us?"[23] He was referring to the horses and cattle which they brought with them and which had died from starvation. In February many of the converts left for the old villages on the Muskingum to gather the grain in their fields that had never been harvested.

On March 4, 1782 a party of 160 militia gathered at the site of Logan's old Mingo town on the west side of the Ohio for the purpose of destroying the Moravian mission villages. Although Cornwallis had surrendered to Washington at Yorktown on October 19, 1781, the war in the West was not abating. There had been three recent attacks on settlers' cabins. They believed the Moravian villages had aided the war parties and that at least some of the attackers had come from the villages. The settlers, inflamed with rage kindled by six years of attacks by war parties that had killed many of their friends and relatives, ached for revenge. In their minds there was no good Indian but a dead Indian. As the militia approached the villages, they observed the Indians working in the fields. They told them to come into town assuring them that they would not be hurt. The Indians were locked in cabins at Gnadenhutten, and after some deliberation, a vote was taken, and it was decided to execute them on the following day. Ninety Christian Indians, twenty-nine men, twenty-seven women, and thirty-four children, courageously singing hymns like the martyr Hus, were led two at a time to the place of execution where their skulls were crushed with a wooden mallet.[24] Those killed included the heart of the mission

---

[23] *Diary of David Zeisberger, A Moravian Missionary Among the Indians of Ohio,* translated and edited by Eugene F. Bliss, 2 vols., Cincinnati: R. Clarke, 1885, Vol 1, pp. 63-64.

[24] The site of the massacre is commemorated by a monument in the memorial park at Gnadenhutten, Ohio. The story of the Moravian mission and massacre is the subject of an outdoor drama at New Philadelephia,

leaders, the men and women who had been with Zeisberger for thirty years. It would be difficult to find people of any race who had lived more devout Christian lives. Following the executions all the buildings in the villages were burned.

As some of the militia returned, they attacked a small band of Delaware who had accepted the Pittsburgh commander's invitation to move close to Pittsburgh for protection and were living on Killbuck Island in the Ohio across from Pittsburgh. One of the Indians killed had a commission in the United States army and had been commended for his valiant service to the nation. It was clear that no Indian was safe among the whites on the Pennsylvania frontier.

News of the massacre at Gnadenhutten quickly spread across the frontier and among the hostile tribes. Among many of the settlers there was satisfaction but fear of retaliation. Among the unconverted Indians there was outrage that these peaceful people who had accepted the white man's religion and led such exemplary lives could be treated in such a manner. It confirmed their conviction that the white man's God had nothing to offer the Indians. Among the colonials in the east there was generally shock and disgust that civilized people could commit such an outrage. The Governor of Pennsylvania demanded an investigation.

The faith of the surviving Christian Indians and their missionaries was sorely tested. Zeisberger wrote:

> This news sank deep into our hearts so that these our brethren, who as martyrs, had all gone to the Savior, were always day and night before our eyes and in our thoughts and we could not forget them, but this in some measure comforted us that they passed to the

Ohio called "Trumpet in the Land" written by Paul Green which has been performed since 1970.

Savior's arms and bosom in such resigned disposition of heart where they will forever rest, protected from the sins and all the wants of the world.[25]

As if God desired to test the limits of the faithful before bringing them to his bosom, immediately before the massacre Zeisberger and the other missionaries received a summons to appear at Half King's Wyandotte village. When they arrived, they appeared before the principal chiefs of the Wyandotte and Delaware tribes where they were presented with a letter from the commander at Detroit. The missionaries and their families were commanded to leave for Detroit. Half King, who considered the missionaries a destabilizing influence in his territory, had informed the Governor that Zeisberger was continuing to send messages to Pittsburgh, and as long as the missionaries were there, they were a threat. After thirty-eight years of work, Zeisberger and his assistants were ordered to abandon their flock. Zeisberger wrote the following:

> Nowhere is a place to be found to which we can retire with our Indians and be secure. The world is already too narrow. From the white people, or so-called Christians, we can hope for no protection, and among the heathen nations also we have no friends left, such outlaws are we! But praise to God, the Lord our God yet lives, who will not forsake us.[26]

---

[25] *Diary of David Zeisberger, A Moravian Missionary Among the Indians of Ohio*, translated and edited by Eugene F. Bliss, 2 vols., Cincinnati: R. Clarke, 1885, Vol 1, p. 81.

[26] *Diary of David Zeisberger, A Moravian Missionary Among the Indians of Ohio*, translated and edited by Eugene F. Bliss, 2 vols., Cincinnati: R. Clarke, 1885, Vol 1, pp. 85-86.

After the missionaries left for Detroit, the Christian Indians abandoned the village on the Sandusky and disbursed among the various tribes in the area. When the missionaries met with the British commander, they learned that he had ordered them to come to Detroit because if he had not complied with the Chiefs' request to remove them, hostile Indians would have killed the missionaries. The Governor said he would send them back to Philadelphia or help them find a safe location for their mission. A location was found on the Huron (now Clinton) River north of Detroit on the land of the Chippewa and word was sent back to the Christian Indians that a new home had been found. They soon began straggling in, but in view of their recent experience, many never returned.

In the meantime an army of 480 frontiersmen under Colonel William Crawford gathered on May 25, 1782, at the site of Logan's former Mingo Town on the west side of the Ohio to begin a march to the Sandusky River to destroy the Wyandotte towns. Crawford was an experienced Indian fighter and friend of President George Washington. David Williamson, who had led the militia against the mission towns, was second in command. The army included many who had participated in the massacre. For years the frontier settlers had urged such an expedition. With the attacks on the settlements increasing, they decided the time had come for a strike that would "kill the viper in his nest." By June 4 they had arrived at the now abandoned Captive Town on the Sandusky where the Christian Indians had spent the terrible winter. That afternoon the warriors of the Wyandotte and Delaware tribes, who had followed the progress of the army since it had left the Ohio, met them. They had sent out a call for reinforcements to the Shawnee and the British at Detroit. The Americans had marched into a trap. They battled until dusk, confident of victory on the following day. Butler's Rangers, a British brigade from Detroit, and warriors from the Shawnee joined the Wyandotte and Delaware warriors the next day. Vastly out numbered and trapped in a small grove of trees surrounded by a tall-grass prairie which concealed the attackers from view, Crawford and his officers determined to wait for nightfall and then attempt to break out and retreat to the Ohio as quickly as possible. Shortly after dark, they organized and began their march. Their plan was quickly discovered, and their column was attacked from all sides. The organized retreat quickly became a rout. Seventy Americans including Colonel Crawford who was captured and burned at the stake, never returned from the expedition. Although the War in the east was over, the bloody War with the Indians in the West would continue intermittently until an army led by General Anthony Wayne defeated them at the Battle of Fallen Timbers near present day Maumee, Ohio in 1794.[27]

The Moravians urged Congress, governing under the Articles of Confederation, to preserve for the Christian Indians the land that had been given to them by the Delaware. In 1785, Congress enacted a law directing the Geographer of the United States, who was authorized to begin surveying land northwest of the Ohio, to reserve the sites of the former Christian Indian towns of Schoenbrunn, Gnadenhutten, and Salem for the exclusive use of the Christian Indians formerly settled there. Colonel Harmar who was stationed at Pittsburgh was authorized to furnish the Christian Indians with 500 bushels of corn, 100 blankets, and other necessaries. The Indian wars that followed the Revolution prevented a survey of the land and the return of the Christian Indians. However, following the conclusion of the Indian Wars with the Treaty of Greenville in 1795, Congress, now governing under the Constitution, in 1796 passed an act granting to the Society of the United Brethren for Propagating the Gospel among the Heathen three 4,000 acre tracts surrounding the sites of the former

---

[27] The site of the battle is commemorated by a state memorial administered by the Ohio Historical Society.

Schoenbrunn, Gnadenhutten, and Salem. The tracts were granted for the sole use of the Christian Indians who were formerly settled there including Killbuck and White Eyes and their descendants. John Ettwein, Bishop of the Moravian Church, had organized the Society. The tracts were surveyed with the assistance of Rufus Putnam, the Surveyor General and founder of Marietta, the first white settlement in Ohio. President John Adams on February 24, 1798, signed the patent transferring ownership of 12,000 acres to the Society for the use of the Christian Indians. The Moravians planned to relocate the Christian Indians who were then living in Canada to the Schoenbrunn tract and lease out the other two tracts to Moravians and their friends so that the Indians would be surrounded with friendly whites who would be supportive of the mission.

In the meantime the Christian Indians who had reassembled with their missionaries in Canada following the abandonment of Captive Town established a village on the Huron River (now Clinton River) north of Detroit on land offered by the Chippewa. They called their new town New Gnadenhutten in memory of their massacred brethren. By 1785 the population of the village had climbed back up to one hundred seventeen. The Chippewa soon became unhappy with the continued presence of the Christian Indians on their land. They had offered it as a temporary refuge, and they felt the continued presence of the guests was interfering with their hunting and fishing. Having heard of the action of Congress reserving land for them at their old sites on the Muskingum and desiring to attract more of their former members who now lived among the Delaware and the Shawnee, the Moravians and their converts made a decision to return to Ohio. They left in the spring of 1786 and hoped to arrive in time to get their crops planted for the current season. The trip took longer than expected, so in late June they stopped at a site of a former Ottawa village on the Cuyahoga River near present day

Cleveland, Ohio, to plant their gardens and fields. Their new village was called Pilgerruh which means Pilgrim's Rest.

On October 7, 1786 Colonel Benjamin Logan led a large army of Kentucky militia in an attack upon the Shawnee towns on the Great Miami and Mad Rivers in western Ohio. The expedition was part of a two-pronged attack planned by George Rogers Clark in retaliation for attacks on Kentucky settlements. While Logan attacked the Shawnee, Clark led an army north against the Miami in the Wabash country in northern Indiana. The first Shawnee village attacked was Mackachack under the leadership of Chief Molunthy who had signed the Great Miami Treaty with the Americans and was told that his people were "included among the friends of the United States." He flew an American flag from a tall pole in front of his house. The Kentuckians approach was discovered, and the Indians began to flee into the woods. The Kentuckians, seeing that they had been discovered, raced into the town on their horses killing a number of women and children and ten men. Lieutenant Ebenezer Denny later reported, "They made no resistance; the men were literally murdered."[28] The Kentuckians then rounded up their captives including Chief Molunthy. Before Logan could restore order, Captain Hugh McGary executed the chief by sinking a tomahawk in his head and scalping him. The Kentuckians burned the village, destroyed the crops, and proceeded north to Wapakoneta where they found that most of the residents had fled. Ten defenders were killed including the chief, and a captive was burned at the stake. Before they were done, eight Shawnee villages and fifteen thousand bushels of corn were destroyed leaving the survivors to face the winter without shelter or food. Eleven warriors, ten chiefs, and a number of women and children were killed, and twenty-six women and

---

[28] R. Douglas Hurt, *The Ohio Frontier, Crucible of the Old Northwest 1720-1830*, Indiana University Press, 1996, p. 99.

two children were captured and taken back to Kentucky. The Americans' action turned the Shawnee into bitter enemies and led to the rise of Tecumseh and his brother the Prophet who organized a confederation of Indians to oppose the Americans during the War of 1812. In view of the increased hostilities, the American commander at Pittsburgh strongly recommended that the missionaries not complete their move to the Muskingum.

In the spring of 1787 the missionaries and Christian Indians moved west to a site on the Pettquotting River near Milan, Ohio, which they named New Salem. They stayed until 1791, building the mission back up to 212 converts. In the meantime tensions and hostilities increased as the American efforts to acquire lands in Ohio for settlement met resistance from most of the Ohio Indians and their western allies. President George Washington's diplomatic efforts to secure the land through treaties failed and so a military effort was launched to secure the Ohio country for white settlement. General Harmar led an expedition north to the Maumee River in northwest Ohio in September 1790. Although a number of Indian villages were destroyed, Harmar's troops were bloodied in two engagements which convinced Harmar to retreat to Fort Washington located at present-day Cincinnati. The Indians considered this a defeat for the Americans, and they were emboldened to continue their attacks on American settlements.

In February 1791, Zeisberger's mission on the Pettquotting received a warning from the Council that the Indians were holding at the forks of the Maumee that the mission must move or risk suffering the same fate that it suffered on the Muskingum. The missionaries received an invitation from Alexander McKee, the British Indian Agent at Detroit, and Matthew Elliott to relocate the mission to tracts of land owned by Elliott and McKee at the mouth of the Detroit River. By May the missionaries and Christian Indians had crossed Lake Erie and were once again building a new village named "die Warte" which means the Watch Tower. The village was located near the present village of Malden Centre, Ontario, and had a view of both the Detroit River and Lake Erie. The mission was now located in a secure location while the battle for Ohio intensified.

General Arthur St. Clair, Governor of the Northwest Territory, was ordered by the President to organize another expedition to attack the Indians in northwest Ohio. He led his army north in September 1791, constructing forts on the way that he named Hamilton and Jefferson. At dawn on November 4, the Indians attacked his army. The Americans suffered their worst defeat from the Indians before or since. Of the fourteen hundred men, six hundred twenty three were killed and two hundred fifty eight wounded. Sixty-nine of one hundred twenty four officers were killed. The American losses surpassed those of any battle during the American Revolution. Despite the defeat President Washington was not ready to abandon the contest for Ohio.

In the meantime the missionaries with the assistance of McKee and Elliott were seeking a permanent location for the mission. During the spring of 1792, the missionaries and their converts found a new site on the Thames River that they named Fairfield. Once again they constructed a new village and cleared land for crops and pasture. While the war for Ohio raged, the new village prospered. Despite the success of the new mission, Zeisberger longed to return to the Muskingum River where he had his greatest success.

Following St. Clair's defeat, Congress authorized an increase in the size of the army to 5,000 and doubled the military budget to $1,000,000. Washington turned to Anthony Wayne, a revolutionary war general with a reputation for tenacity, discipline, and aggressiveness. Wayne took his time gathering and training his army near Pittsburgh. The army was then moved to Cincinnati. After diplomatic efforts again failed, the army marched north. Wayne established his headquarters at Fort Greenville and then built another fort at the site of St. Clair's defeat called Fort Recovery. He proceeded very deliberately and carefully, never allowing an opportunity for a surprise attack. In the meantime the British to show their support for the Indians constructed a fort at the rapids of the Maumee called Fort Miami near present day Perrysburg. On August 20, 1794, the Americans defeated the Indians at the Battle of Fallen Timbers, and when the Indians sought refuge in the British fort, they were denied assistance. The Indians now realized that they stood alone against the Americans, and they simply did not have the forces to match Wayne's army. On August 13, 1795, the Indians signed the Treaty of Greenville giving up any claim to land in Ohio east and south of the treaty line. Two thirds of Ohio was ceded to the whites. After years of warfare, southern and eastern Ohio was now safe for white settlement.

Following the Treaty, the Moravians were now able to proceed with the survey of the three four thousand acre tracts on the Muskingum which the Government had reserved for the Christian Indians. In the spring of 1798 the Moravian mission Board sent John Heckewelder and Benjamin Mortimer to inform Zeisberger that the survey of the tracts on the Muskingum had been completed, and the land was ready for the Christian Indians to return. In August Zeisberger, who was now 77 years old, and his wife and his assistant Mortimer with 39 converts made the trip to the Muskingum. On October 7 they arrived at the site of the new mission on the Schoenbrunn tract that they named Goshen. In addition to the mission run by Zeisberger, the Moravians established a new white town named Gnadenhutten at the site of the massacre. This town was placed under the leadership of John Heckewelder. It was to be populated by Moravians and was to house the trading post where the Christian Indians could exchange their furs, baskets, meats and other goods produced by them for eastern products. Goshen was to become a training ground for white missionaries and Christian Indian helpers who would be sent west to establish new missions among the Indians.

When the Goshen mission and Gnadenhutten were established, the nearest white village was 65 miles away on the east side of the Ohio River. Ohio was uninhabited by white settlers except for a ten mile strip along the west side of the Ohio River. It seemed that the mission would be protected from the bad influence of living near whites and drinking Indians. However, the coming years would see a rapid influx of white settlement around the mission and with it the temptation of liquor.

Following the signing of the Treaty of Greenville, most of the Delaware settled on the White River in Indiana. They included many who had formerly lived at the missions on the Muskingum. In 1800 the chief of the Delaware sent an invitation to the Christian Indians at Goshen to join them. The following year two missionaries and thirteen of the Indians from Goshen moved to the White River to establish a mission there. The missionaries stayed for five years, most of which were spent in fear for their lives. During the final year they witnessed the chief who had invited them tomahawked by his son and thrown into a fire built in the center of town. Joshua, the last male Christian Indian living at the mission who came with the party from Goshen in 1801, suffered the same fate, as did one of the old women who had lived in the missions most of her life. They were the victims of the Delaware's version of the Salem witch trials.

There was much illness and death among the Delaware and the other Indians in 1805. Young Delaware braves were unhappy with their leaders who had entered into a treaty with Indiana Governor William Henry Harrison that traded land for peace. There were two traditional explanations for their unhappy situation. First, that the Great Spirit was punishing them because they had been bad, and second, that witches, who were empowered by the evil one, were poisoning people. A Delaware woman, who had been baptized by the Moravians as a child but separated from them long ago, had a vision that the illness was due to the Great Spirit's anger at the Indians for their sinfulness and their neglect of traditional ceremonies that appeased the spirits. A prophet would be sent to show them correct conduct. They must listen because a great storm was coming. The wicked would be destroyed. Witches were using the power given to them by the evil one to poison people. The Prophet, brother of Tecumseh, Shawnees living near the Delaware on White River, claimed to have similar visions. He added Heaven to his vision as the reward for those who followed his teaching and Hell as punishment for those who didn't. The Prophet said Indians must throw away their traditional medicine bags and follow him as the spokesman for the Great Spirit. He emphasized that Indians must preserve their traditional values, ceremonies, and lands. They must reject the white man's culture and isolate themselves from its influence. He prophesied that the white man would be destroyed by the Great Spirit. The Prophet was a highly emotional speaker who convinced many Indians that he had a message which explained their suffering and offered hope for them if they would restore their traditional values. He claimed the power to identify the witches who were causing illness among the Indians. He was invited to the Delaware village by the angry young braves to identify the witches which were causing the illness in their village and causing them to lose their land. The Prophet identified the chief, Joshua and the others who were executed as witches. In this climate of hysteria and hatred of anything which challenged traditional beliefs and ceremonies and search for scapegoats, the Moravians decided to withdraw the mission. The shrieks of hate and anger had once again drowned out their gentle voice of compassion.

Now that peace had arrived, the Moravians decided to reestablish their mission at New Salem on the Pettquotting River near present day Milan, Ohio. When established in the spring of 1804, the mission drew on converts from Fairfield and Goshen for their seed congregation and a missionary trained at Goshen. The following year a treaty was made at Fort Industry at present-day Toledo, Ohio, whereby the Americans purchased the land where the mission was located. No land was reserved for the mission and within a few years the land surrounding the mission had been purchased by whites. The mission continued until 1809 when the remaining residents returned to Fairfield and Goshen.

Ignatius and Christina were among the most respected and loyal converts at the Goshen mission. They were baptized in 1773 and for thirty-two years had remained loyal to Zeisberger and the mission program. They were by his side through all the moves and trials of this difficult period. They were industrious, hard working, moral, and fully committed to the Savior. Zeisberger was there when their son Henry was baptized and watched him while he grew up. He was a difficult, rebellious teenager, and had caused his parents many disappointments. On March 30, 1805, Henry committed suicide by taking poison. He simply could not reconcile the conflict between the two cultures in which he grew up. Zeisberger believed the boy had committed an unforgivable sin. He refused permission for him to be buried in the mission cemetery and refused to give him a Christian funeral. The heart broken parents buried their son in the hills without a Christian burial and without their best friend Zeisberger present. They had faithfully done everything that they had been taught to live good Christian lives. They had put their trust in and suffered for the Lord. Now they faced the excruciating thought that their beloved son was condemned to eternal damnation. The family and their friends felt that their beloved eighty three year old missionary had abandoned them at a critical time in their lives. He seemed like the unforgiving God of the Old Testament rather than the gentle Teacher on the Mount preaching love and forgiveness. Their faith was tested. They rebelled in anguish and anger. Most of the congregation purchased liquor from two merchants in New Philadelphia and spent Easter weekend in a drunken revelry. In May Ignatius and his family left the mission. In July Ignatius died. The drunkenness in the congregation continued. Although conditions improved at the Mission, it never returned to the sanguine days before Henry's death. The suicide had been the final test for the old missionary.

During his final days the Christian Indians came to Zeisberger's cabin and sang hymns from the hymnal he had prepared for them. His final day is recorded in the entry for November 17, 1808, of the mission diary:

> Zeisberger lay calm without pain and perfectly conscious. The converts sang hymns, treating of Jesus, the Prince of Life, of death swallowed up in victory; and of Jerusalem, the Church above. He occasionally responded by signs expressive of peace and joy. Amid such strains at half past three o:clock in the afternoon, he breathed his last, without a struggle and went to God. All present immediately fell on their knees.[29]

Zeisberger was buried among his beloved Christian Indians at the mission cemetery.

The Moravian missions were tested by still another war. In Ohio America's second war with Britain was like the first, primarily an Indian War. Like the first, it stirred up the old hate and anger between whites and Indians. At the

---

[29] Goshen Diary, November 17, 1808, Moravian Archives, Bethlehem, Pa., Box 171, Trans in William N. Schwarze, "Characteristics and Achievements of David Zeisberger", *Ohio Archaelogical and Historical Society Publications* Vol 18 (1909) p. 195.

beginning of hostilities, Detroit under the command of General William Hull was surrounded by the British under General Brock and Indian allies under Tecumseh. After a few days of fighting, Hull surrendered in a humiliating defeat for which he was later court martialed. With the news of Hull's surrender, fear of raids by Indian war parties swept across the Ohio frontier. In New Philadelphia located a few miles north of the Goshen mission, hostility toward Indians reached a boiling point. A county official, a friend and supporter of the mission, wrote to the missionary Benjamin Mortimer, strongly suggesting that they move east, as he could no longer guarantee their safety. "Humanity cries aloud for the hand of protection to be extended to the innocent Indians who have submitted their all to the protection of the U. States, but I am sorry to state that I have no difficulty in saying that in my opinion they will not remain undisturbed in their present place of residence."[30] Mortimer, who had served the mission since the Christian Indians returned to the Muskingum from Canada, invited the town to send white men to stay at the village to serve as guards and spies. They would be able to report back to the town what they observed and dispel rumors that the Christian Indians were hostile or were harboring hostile Indians. The plan worked and an attack on the village was avoided.

On October 5, 1813, the War in the West reached its climax at "Moraviantown" on the Thames in Ontario, Canada. This was the Moravian mission of Fairfield founded by Zeisberger. Here the Christian Indians lived who had not returned with Zeisberger to the Muskingum in 1798. Remembering the fate of their friends and relatives who were massacred at Gnadenhutten, they had remained in Canada

[30] Earl P. Olmstead, *Blackcoats Among the Delaware*, Kent State University Press, 1991, p. 168, citing Moravian Church Archives, box 173, folder 9, p. 31.

thinking that they lived in a location that was safe from conflict. 150 of them lived in a village with nearly fifty houses and a church. They had cleared about two hundred acres surrounding the village where they grew their corn and pastured their livestock.

Following the abandonment of Detroit and Fort Malden across the river from Detroit, the British under the leadership of General Procter and the Indians under the leadership of Tecumseh retreated up the Thames pursued by the Americans under the leadership of General William Henry Harrison. The British and their Indian allies made their stand just below Moraviantown. The initial American charge over ran the British position and sent Procter fleeing for safety. Vastly outnumbered, the Indians faced the Americans alone. Tecumseh had spent years trying to unite the tribes to defend their lands. He would not consider surrender or retreat. The Kentucky frontiersmen who made up the brunt of Harrison's army were fired with a desire to avenge earlier losses at the River Raisin and Fort Meigs.[31] Brave men threw themselves against each other in a ferocious struggle. For a while it seemed that the Indians might hold, then Tecumseh fell. The leader, who many of his followers believed was protected by the Great Spirit, was dead. With Tecumseh's death the Indians' hope of stopping the white man's advance evaporated. His surviving followers disappeared into the woods and swamps. Following the battle Moraviantown was totally destroyed by the American army. With winter approaching the Christian Indians were once again deprived of shelter and food.[32] Once again, the Christian Indians and their

[31] Fort Meigs is a state memorial at Perrysburg, Ohio, operated by the Ohio Historical Society. The story of Fort Meigs is found in Larry R. Nelson, *Men of Patriotism, Courgage & Enterprise, Fort Meigs in the War of 1812*, Heritage Books, 1985.

[32] The incident was reported to Congress in "Memorial and Petition of John G. Cunow, acting on behalf of the Moravian Church dated February

missionary leaders, who simply wanted to be left alone to live their lives in accordance with their Savior's message of love and compassion, saw their work smashed by a world consumed by hate. Once again, they remembered the suffering of their Savior and his apostles. Praising the Lord, they relocated across the river and built the mission village that they called New Fairfield. This remained a Moravian mission until 1903, when it was turned over to the Methodists. Today it is still inhabited by descendants of the Christian Indians.[33]

In 1821 part of the Christian Indians left for the mission at New Fairfield and the last of the missionaries left Goshen for Bethlehem, leaving nineteen or twenty Indians at the mission who were attended by the minister of a small congregation of the Moravian Church nearby. The following year Church leaders presented a report to the Secretary of War and Congress on the history and present status of the mission and a recommendation that it be relieved of responsibility for the three tracts which had been deeded to it for the Christian Indians.[34] Congress appointed an agent to negotiate an agreement with the Moravians and the Christian Indians to relinquish their land. An agreement was reached, and on August 26, 1824, Congress passed a law implementing the agreement. The land was returned to the United States, and its

---

10, 1814," a copy of which may be found at the library of the Ohio Historical Society.

[33] The tribe is known as the Moravian on the Thames Band. The subsequent history of this band and other remnants of the Delaware Indians is found in C. A. Weslager, The Delaware Indians, A History, Rutgers University Press, New Brunswick, N.J. 1972

[34] The report is found in "Message of the President of the United States transmitting information in relation to certain Christian Indians and the lands intended for their benefit on the Muskingum in the State of Ohio granted under an Act of Congress of June 1, 1796 to the Society of United Brethren for Propagating the Gospel among the Heathen dated December 10, 1822." A copy may be found at the Library of the Ohio Historical Society.

sale was authorized. The Christian Indians who still lived on the Thames were given the right to 24,000 acres in the West if they should decide in the future that they wished to go there.

Despite the best of intentions the Moravians were simply not able to operate a successful mission surrounded by whites. They were not successful in attracting Moravian residents in sufficient numbers to protect the Christian Indians from the bad influences of white culture, and few Christian Indians felt safe living at a mission surrounded by whites who had killed so many of their relatives and friends.

CHAPTER 6

TRIUMPH OF COMPASSION OVER HATE

On June 5, 1872, a 35 foot tall monument was dedicated at the memorial park in Gnadenhutten, Ohio, near the site of the massacre. The monument reads, "Here triumphed in death ninety Christian Indians March 8, 1782." The Bishop of the Moravian Church from Bethlehem gave the address and four Delaware Indians descended from the martyrs participated in the unveiling. Music was provided by the Moravian Church and by the trombone choir from Bethlehem, Pennsylvania. Ten thousand people attended the dedication.

An inquiry into the massacre was ordered by the Governor Moore of Pennsylvania and reports rendered by the Washington County lieutenant Col. James Marshel who authorized the expedition and Col. David Williamson who commanded it. No record of those reports remains. General William Irvine, the commander at Pittsburgh confided to the Governor that "it will be almost impossible to obtain a just account of the conduct of the militia at Muskingum" because none of those who were present would testify. He was of the opinion "further inquiry into this matter will not only be fruitless, but in the end may be attended with disagreeable consequences."[35] No court martial was ever held or person charged with the murders of the Christian Indians. No one ever publicly admitted his participation in the murders.

The story of the Moravians shows three ways people react to suffering and hostility. The first is by hate, anger and violence. This reaction appeared time and time again in this story. It was the predominant force of history during the time period covered. The story shows that this reaction inevitably led to more suffering and more hate, anger and violence in an endless cycle of misery. The second reaction to suffering is withdrawal from the world. Among the Indians in this story withdrawal frequently took the form of alcohol abuse, depression or simply low self esteem which sapped motivation. The third reaction is compassion. The Moravians who had a long history of suffering for their faith turned their suffering into compassion for the suffering of others. When surrounded by hostility, they did not react with anger, hate and violence. They proved that people can choose another way.

Christ suffered on the cross and taught love and compassion not hate, anger and violence. His Father in Heaven did not react to the torture and death of his Son by destroying the human race or even those who particpated in His execution. The disciples of Jesus did not become consumed by a desire for revenge. They taught love and forgiveness not hate and revenge. The Moravian missionaries and their Christian Indian converts followed this teaching and showed by their lives the highest potential for mankind. Like Jesus, they were compassionate revolutionaries. As shown by their story, mankind will never escape suffering. It is the fate of all to die and experience the death of loved-ones; to suffer misfortune and disappointment; to want more than is received; to realize that all the worldy strivings and pretensions of men

---

[35] C.W. Butterfield, *Washington-Irvine Correspondence*, Madison, Wisonsin: David Atwood, 1882, pp. 241-242.

and women will turn to dust. This is the common fate of humanity. What the Moravians showed is that people have the freedom and the power to choose how they react to suffering and violence. Rather than reacting with hate, anger, and violence, or withdrawal and self-destruction, people can choose to react with compassion for the suffering of others, even their enemies.

The monument to the massacred Indians at Gnadenhutten celebrates the hope and commitment that through suffering and death love and compassion will ultimately triumph over hate, anger and violence. The Moravian missionaries dedicated their lives to that hope and commitment. Although they met with limited success because of the formidable odds against them, their lives shine as a beacons in the night showing the path to the highest potential for mankind.

CHAPTER 7

THE PRESIDENT'S MORAVIAN ANCESTORS

The President's connection with the Moravian missionaries is through the Demuth family. The first Moravian ancestor of whom there is a record is Christoph Demuth. According to a family historian, he was a magistrate at a village in Moravia, now part of the Czech Republic. He and his family were identified with the "hidden seed" of the ancient Unitas Fratrum previous to its renewal at Herrnhut in 1727.[36] Christoph, born in the 1650s, and his wife Elizabeth had several children and grandchildren who were involved with the renewal, organization and early history of the Moravian Church in Europe and America. A grandson Gottleib Demuth was among the first Moravian missionaries sent to America and was among the early residents of Bethlehem, Pennsylvania. A great grandson by the name, Christoph Demuth, was among the first Moravian settlers in Ohio, bringing his family to Gnadenhutten in 1803, the year Ohio was admitted to the union. The President is descended from these Demuths through his mother Barbara Bush. The

---

[36] C. F. Battershell, *The Demuth Family and the Moravian Church*, New Philadelphia, 1931, p.4 Copy available at the Family History Library of the Church of Jesus Christ Latter Day Saints at Salt Lake City, Utah and the Tuscarawas County Genelogical Society, Dennison, Ohio.

village where the Demuths lived is referred to in a list of emigrants to Herrnhut as Kadelsdorf (Karlsdorf) near Krulich on the borders of Bohemia.[37]

The first member of the family to arrive at Herrnhut was Johann Christoph Demuth, son of Christoph and Elizabeth, born November 6, 1689, at Karlsdorf. He was also known as Christoph and to avoid confusion will be referred to as Christoph II. A boxmaker by trade, he, like Christian David, was an evangelical lay preacher who traveled extensively spreading the news of the establishment of the Christian community at Herrnhut and encouraging others to join. He was no doubt instrumental in causing his brother and sisters, nieces and nephews to come to Herrnhut.

The following memoir published following his death tells his remarkable story:

> Christoph Demuth, a manufacturer of paper boxes, came from Moravia. In 1726, being greatly troubled in spirit and longing for peace, he forsook his home, and by a wonderful leading of Providence, came to Herrnhut. Apparently he had not decided where to go, nor had he heard anything of Count Zinzendorf, nor of the refuge there offered by him for refugees from Moravia. A few weeks later he returned to Moravia for his wife and two children. Brother Demuth was present at the communion at Berthelsorf on August 13, 1727, and was a participant. In 1726 in company with

---

[37] *Transactions of the Moravian Historical Society Vol 9, Parts 1 and 2*, 1911, pp. 71, 72. Battershell refers to the name of the village as Karlsdorf. Reichcigl refers to it as Karlov. The gravemarker of Christian II refers to it as Cathelsdorf. Dr. Stephen Paczolt, Sr. Technical Information Specialist, Reference Section, Geography and Map Division of the Library of Congress is of the opinion that the village was called called Karlsdorf and is now known as Moravsky Karlov which is located at 50 deg. 2 min N; 16 deg. 47 min E.

Christian David, he went to Moravia, remaining there six weeks, and although in danger of imprisonment, visited devout souls in various places, who in their concealment, were longing for freedom to worship the Lord according to the dictates of their consciences and to enjoy the spiritual blessings which their fathers of the Brethren's Church had so highly prized. Living in Herrnhut, and supporting himself by the labor of his hands, he made many journeys in the cause of the Lord. Among the rest, he went to Berlin in 1729, to various portions of Prussia in 1732, in company with Frederick Boehnish, to Wurtemberg in 1730, in order to accompany two young women from Switzerland to Herrnhut.

In 1743 together with 120 others he and his family came to Pennsylvania, later serving in Muhlbach, Germantown, and Fredericktown as minister. He was an excellent singer, and when preaching to the people, he often proclaimed the gospel in song, which was edifying and impressive, as was also his devout walk ("priesterlicher Wandel") During the greater part of this time, Nazareth was his home, where "his example of holy living was not without blessed fruits." On the last day of his life, though with a feeble voice, he frequently repeated his favorite hymn, "Jesu Kreuze, Jesu Todesstunden, Jesu, uber alles schone Wunden, Jesu, Gottes-Leichelein, Soll mein Ein und Alles sein." Two of his children survived him: Ferdinand and a daughter married to Peter Thiel. His age was 64 years, 3 months and 20 days.[38]

---

[38] *Transactions of the Moravian Historical Society*, Vol 7, Part 3, 1904, p. 90.

According to the diary of the Moravian congregations at Berlin and Rixdorf, they first learned of the establishment of Herrnhut as a result of a visit from Christian David and Christoph II in 1726.[39] According to a record kept of emigrants to Herrnhut, he arrived in September 1726, and he brought his wife from Moravia to Herrnhut in November 1726.[40] He is among fifty Moravians who are commemorated on a monument at Nazareth.

Christoph II was married to Anna Marie Schmidt in 1716. Her husband brought her and the children to Herrnhut in November 1726, and she accompanied him to America in 1743. She died in Nazareth in March 1761. Their children included Regina, Hans Joseph, Ann, Ferdinand, Anna, and Johann Martin. Regina married Peter Diehl (Thiel). Only Ferdinand and Regina survived. Ferdinand died August 30, 1768, at Herrnhut, Saxony.[41]

Christoph II's sister Justina also came to Herrnhut in 1726, no doubt through the encouragement of her brother. She lived and worked as a single sister at Herrnhut until her death in 1732.[42]

Christoph II's brother in law Christian Wetzel, known as the "boardcutter" emigrated to Herrnhut in 1728 after imprisonment at Eisenberg. He was from Weiswasser near

---

[39] J. Taylor Hamilton and Kenneth G. Hamilton, *History of the Moravian Church, 1922-1957*, Interprovincial Board of Christian Education, Moravian Church of America, 1967, p. 14.

[40] *Transactions of the Moravian Historical Society* Vol 9, Parts 1 and 2, 1911, p. 71.

[41] *Transactions of the Moravian Historical Society* Vol 9, Parts 1 and 2, 1911, p. 71. Ferdinand's date of death was obtained from James Shaffer.

[42] *Transactions of the Moravian Historical Society* Vol 9, Parts 1 and 2, 1911, p. 73 Batterfield refers to her as Justine, a male. Both Butterfield and Rechcigl state he/she arrived in 1726.

Grulich in Bohemia. Christoph II brought his sister Maria Magdalena Wetzel and her five children to Herrnhut in 1730.[43]

Christoph II's brother Gotthard arrived at Herrnhut in 1727. On January 10, 1728, he married Regina Leopold. She had arrived at Herrnhut on March 10, 1727, with her mother Elizabeth, brothers Augustin and Tobias, and sisters Rosina and Anna Maria.[44] Gotthard was sent to Georgia with the first group of Moravian missionaries to the American colonies in 1735. In one record he is described as a watchmaker and in another as a joiner.[45] His wife was sent with the second group the following year and brought with her Gotthard's nephew Gottleib Demuth, age 20.[46]

As a result of the controversy over military service, Gotthard, Regina, and their nephew Gottlieb left Georgia in January, 1738 and settled in Germantown, Pennsylvania.[47] Germantown had been established by Dutch Quakers and German Mennonites near Philadelphia in 1683. By 1738, it was a well-established community and included German-speaking people from a variety of countries.

Gotthard's assistance with the establishment of the Moravian communities at Bethlehem and Nazareth can be gleaned from entries in the diaries which were kept at Bethlehem:

---

[43] *Transactions of the Moravian Historical Society* Vol 9, Parts 1 and 2, 1911, p. 73

[44] *Transactions of the Moravian Historical Society* Vol 9, Parts 1 and 2, 1911, p. 71, 72.

[45] E. Merton Coulter and Albert B. Saye, *A List of the Early Settlers of Georgia*, University of Georgia Press, 1949, reprinted for Clearfield Company by Genealogical Publishing Co., Inc. 1996 p. 14; Adelaide L. Fries, *The Moravians in Georgia*, Edwards & Broughton, Raleigh, 1905, p. 48.

[46] Adelaide L. Fries, *The Moravians in Georgia*, Edwards & Broughton, Raleigh, 1905, p. 91, 92.

[47] Adelaide L. Fries, *The Moravians in Georgia*, Edwards & Broughton, Raleigh, 1905, pp. 187, 188.

July 15, 1741 Gotthard Demuth and David Tanneberger visited from Germantown and on July 17 left for home.

September 24, 1741 Gotthard Demuth who had been working for us during the summer returned from a visit to his family and resumed work.[48]

At the time of the first entry the Moravians who had wintered at the Whitefield tract had just moved to the Allen tract due to Whitefield's order cancelling the transaction and were constructing the first buildings at what was to become Bethlehem. Bethlehem was located about 60 miles north of Germantown, several days away by horse-drawn wagon. The second entry shows that he had been assisting with construction of the first buildings at Bethlehem.

In December 1741 Count Zinzendorf arrived in New York and then proceeded to Philadelphia. He no doubt stayed with the Moravians in Germantown before proceeding to Bethlehem. It is very likely that Gotthard accompanied Zinsendorf's party and was present at the Christmas eve service when Bethlehem was named. Zinzendorf then returned to Germantown where he preached at the Reformed Church there and held the first synod there with representatives of the other German-speaking churches. On March 25, 1742, Zinzendorf organized the Moravian congregation at Germantown. On April 17, it was decided to open a boarding school at Germantown based on the Moravian model in Europe. On April 18 and May 16 additional synods were held in Germantown.[49] Since Gotthard Demuth was one of a

---

[48] William C. Reichel, Editor, *Memorials of the Moravian Church* Vol 1, Philadlephia, 1870, pp. 169, 172.
[49] William C. Reichel, Editor, *Memorials of the Moravian Church* Vol 1, Philadelphia, 1870 pp. 181-183.

handful of Moravian residents in Germantown at the time, it is highly likely that he was involved with these events.
The following entry is recorded in the diary:

> June 6, 1742 In the afternoon of June 6, all of the brethren and sisters who had recently arrived from Europe proceeded to Germantown and had a very blessed love feast in Theoboldt Endt's new home. It was here that the first synod had been held at the beginning of the year. And also the brethren and sisters were accustomed to break their journey here since it was occupied by Gotthard Demuth and Augustin Niesser.[50]

On June 14, 1742, the congregation at Bethlehem was organized into bands and classes and Gotthard and Regina Demuth were listed in a class of married people under leaders Johannes Brandemiller and Rosina Nitschmann.[51] The following additional entries appear in the diary:

> June 17, 1742 Two wagons arrived herewith ... Gotthard Demuth and wife Regina ... together with boarding school children from Germantown.

> June 28, 1742 Gotthard Demuth returned to Germantown after several days visit.

> July 9, 1742 Bishop David Nitschmann arrived from his visit to St. Thomas with Gotthard Demuth from Germantown.

---

[50] Kenneth G. Mamilton, *The Bethlehem Diary, Vol 1, 1742-1744*, Bethlehem, 1871 p. 14.
[51] Kenneth G. Hamilton, *The Bethlehem Diary*, Vol 1, 1742-1744, Bethlehem, 1971 p. 18.

April 28, 1743 Gotthard Demuth arrived to construct the mill.

June 20, 1743 After helping construct the mill, Gotthard Demuth returned to Germantown.

June 23, 1744 Gotthard Demuth came to inspect and repair the saw mill. Returned home after six days.[52]

Gotthard died on December 11, 1744. August Spangenberg, who had come with him to Georgia in 1735 and who now led the community at Bethlehem preached at Gotthard's funeral.[53] Gotthard was survived by his widow Regina and two sons, age 3 and 7. On December 26, 1744, she arrived at Bethlehem where she was to remain with her children.[54] Regina married David Tanneberger on June 19, 1747 at Bethlehem.[55] Tanneberger, a shoemaker, had come to Georgia on the same boat with Regina and had also lived in Germantown.[56]

Gotthard's youngest son Christian Frederick Demuth, born December 26, 1741, died at the Moravian settlement at Hope, New Jersey September 10, 1781, shortly after his marriage to Magdalena Stotz on March 14, 1781.[57] Hope was a Moravian settlement established in 1768 which flourished for sometime before disbanding in 1808.

Gotthard and Regina's oldest son Johann Christoph Demuth, born September 19, 1738, was a tobacco and snuff

---

[52] Kenneth G. Hamilton, *The Bethlehem Diary* Vol 1, 1742-1744, Vol 1, Bethlehem, 1971.

[53] Kenneth G. Hamilton, *The Bethlehem Diary* Vol 1, 1742-1744, Vol 1, Bethlehem, 1971.

[54] Kenneth G. Hamilton, *The Bethlehem Diary* Vol 1, 1742-1744, Vol 1, Bethlehem, 1971, p. 215.

[55] Marriage Register, Moravian Church, Bethlehem, p. 112. .

[56] Adelaide L. Fries, *The Moravians in Georgia,* Edwards & Broughton, Raleigh, 1905, pp. 92, 238.

[57] Marriage Register Moravian Church, Bethlehem, p. 112

dealer in Lancaster, Pennsylvania from 1770 to 1816.[58] His shop located at 114 East King Avenue is now the oldest operating tobacco shop in America. Adjacent to the shop is the Demuth home which is maintained as a museum honoring Charles Demuth, 1883-1935, famous American painter who was a descendant of Johann Christoph Demuth. Charles did much of his painting at the home.[59]

The President is descended from Christoph and Elizabeth's oldest son Tobias Demuth who died in Moravia in 1715 at the age of 35, leaving his widow Rosina with five children. Some believe Tobias suffered a martyr's death because of his religious beliefs, which would explain the commitment of his widow and children. While still living in Moravia, Tobias' widow Rosina in 1728 hosted a religious meeting attended by two of the Brethren from Herrnhut.[60] As a result she and her daughter Veronica and son Josef were jailed where they endured many hardships for over a year. They were freed on bail in order to resume their farm work and found an opporunity to escape. Abandoning all their possessions, she and her daughter Veronica made their way to Herrnhut in 1729.[61] Rosina died there September 27, 1732.

---

[58] Franklin Ellis and Samuel Evans, *History of Lancaster County, Pa.* 1883 p. 369; *Pennsylvania Archives* 3rd Ser. Vol 17 p. 456, 604, 755.

[59] For information on Charles Demuth, the Demuth Museum and the Tobacco Shop go to the web page of the Demuth Foundation at www.demuth.org.

[60] Memorial of Johann Bohner, Bethlehem History Project, http://bdhp.moravian.edu/personal_papers

[61] This account is from Miloslav Rechcigl Jr., "Another Visit to Moravian Demuths", *Demuth/DeMuth Newsletter*, No. 21, pp. 208-209. A slightly different account in found in C. F. Battershell, *The Demuth Family and the Moravian Church*, New Philadelphia, 1931, p.5. He states, "About 1728 his widow Rosina and her eldest son Joseph were thrown into prison in Moravia and held there for over a year, suffering severely on account of starvation, cold, vermin and general mistreatment, until finally their jailer became drunk and they managed to escape."

Christoph II brought Rosina's children Joseph, Gottleib, Anna Rosina, and Anna Maria to Herrnhut in June 1730.[62]

Tobias and Rosina's daughter Veronica married Valentin Loehans and the two of them served as missionaries to black slaves on St. Thomas in the West Indies. After his death in 1743, she married John Boehner. They served at St. Thomas until 1765 when they moved to the mission at St. John. She died of a fever shortly thereafter. Because of her love and concern, she was beloved by the black women she served. When her death was announced to the congregation at St. Thomas, they broke out in weeping.[63]

After Tobias and Rosina's daughter Anna Marie came to Herrnhut, she lived with the family of Count Zinzendorf. She was ordained a deaconess. In 1738 she became the wife of Rev. Anton A. Lawatsch. She served in the capacity of "general elder" or spiritual adviser to the female members of the Church. After coming to Pennsylvania in 1752, she assisted in the founding of Lititz, and in 1757 led a group of newly married persons to the Moravian settlements at Wachovia. She died in 1760 at Bethlehem.[64]

Tobias' and Rosina's son Josef married Judith Schaul, a converted jewess, and stayed in Europe, where he died November 27, 1783 at Zeist. His daughter Agnes and her husband George Matthew Loesche were missionaries at the Moravian missionary in Surinam, South America. When

[62] *Transactions of the Moravian Historical Society* Vol 9, Parts 1 and 2, 1911, p. 71, 72.

[63] Miloslav Rechcigl Jr., "Another Visit to Moravian Demuths", *Demuth/DeMuth Newsletter*, No. 21, p. 209.

[64] Miloslav Rechcigl Jr., "Another Visit to Moravian Demuths", *Demuth/DeMuth Newsletter*, No. 21, p. 209

forced to retire due to poor health, they moved to Bethlehem. Agnes died January 3, 1832, and is buried there.[65]

Tobias and Rosina's daughter Anna Rosina was a deaconess. She married a Hintz and died at the Moravian settlement of Herrnhag in 1745.[66]

President Bush is descended from Tobias' and Rosina's son Gottlieb who arrived at Hernnhut in June, 1730, with his brother Josef and sisters Anna Rosina and Anna Marie. Gottlieb was born the year his father died. He was fifteen when he arrived at Herrnhut. He came to Georgia with his aunt Regina with the second group of Moravian missionaries who arrived in 1736. The group also included the Zeisbergers, parents of David, the missionary to the Indians. David joined them later so Gottleib no doubt knew David Zeisberger well. Gottleib was with the group that John Wesley described as fearless during a terrible storm. When the decision was made to abandon the mission in Georgia, he left with his aunt and uncle for Germantown, Pennsylvania in January 1738. He married Eva Gutsler, widow of Henry Hehl, the following year. His particpation in the establishment of Bethelehem and Nazareth is shown by the following diary entries:

> August 3, 1742 Gottleib Demuth in the process of moving here, began to store his furniture with us.

> August 5, 1742 Gottleib Demuth and wife moved to Bethlehem from neighboring area.

---

[65] Miloslav Rechcigl Jr., "Another Visit to Moravian Demuths", *Demuth/DeMuth Newsletter*, No. 21, p. 209; C. F. Battershell, *The Demuth Family and the Moravian Church*, New Philadelphia, 1931, p.6.
[66] C. F. Battershell, *The Demuth Family and the Moravian Church*, New Philadelphia, 1931, p.6

August 8, 1742 House to be built for Gottleib Demuth this week by all hands. The house which Gottleib Demuth is to build should be provided with two rooms, one for him, the other for persons who may become ill.

August 9, 1742 Gottleib Demuth's house begun today.

November 24, 1742 Construction of washhouse to begin; carpenters include Gottleib Demuth.

January 30, 1743 Gottleib Demuth moved to Nazareth with wife and child and little James.

April 16, 1743 Gottleib Demuth went to Philadelphia.

June 22, 1743 Gottleib Demuth's wife delivered son; baptized that evening by Brother Kohn; Brothrs Anton, Huber, Nitschman, Seidel and Bischoff are godfathers.

July 18, 1743 Brother Franke left with the children who are to live in Nazareth including Gottleib Demuth's son.

September 15, 1743 Following the address, Brother Nitschman prayed over those newly received, which included Gottleib Demuth.

April 10, 1744 A communion love feast was held which the congregation observed with inexpressable emotion; there were 144 who communed. Among them sister Eva Demuth who partook for the first time.[67]

[67] Kenneth G. Hamilton, *The Bethlehem Diary* Vol 1, 1742-1744, Bethlehem, 1971.

After living for a while at Fredricktown and Shoeneck, Gottleib moved to Allemangel in Lynn Township, Lehigh County, which was located on the frontier. In July 1742 Count Zinzendorf had spent the night there and preached to neighboring settlers. A small Moravian congregation was organized. A school house was completed in January, 1747, which also was used as the church. Gottleib was issued a warrant for 95 acres there on August 24, 1753.[68] His son Christoph was born August 27, 1755 and baptized at the Allemangel Moravian Church.[69] Following the outbreak of the French and Indian War the setlers in the area were subjected to repeated attacks. A diary kept by one of the residents of the area recorded the following incidents:

Jan 4, 1756 Four men killed in fight with Indians
Feb 5, 1756 15 Persons murdered by 12 Indians. Three or four plantions burned
March 6, 1756 Woman and two children murdered by Indians
March 22, 1756 Man and wife murdered
March 24, 1756 Man murdered
March 28, 1756 Man murdered
June 22, 1756 Man killed[70]

On October 31, 1755, thirty settlers took refuge in the schoolhouse to escape a war party. On March 12, 1756, forty-three men, women and children from Allemangel arrived at Bethlehem seeking refuge.[71]

---

[68] Charles Rhoads Roberts, *History of Lehigh County* Vol 1 p. 810.
[69] Baptism Record, Allemangel Moravian Congregation in Lynn Township 1745-1770..
[70] Charles Rhoads Roberts, *History of Lehigh County*, Pa.Vol 3, p. 1462, citing the Diary of David Scultze.
[71] Extracted from minutes of Penna Synod of Moravian Church

Gottleib and his family moved back to Shoeneck, which was located about a mile from Nazareth. He had acquired 50 acres there by survey dated August 24, 1753, which was the same date as he acquired the land at Allemangel.[72] He acquired an additional 15 acres on November 30, 1753.[73] Shoeneck was in the midst of the farms that produced the farm products to support the Moravian communities at Nazareth and Bethlehem and the missionary program. The record indicates Gottlieb worked for the Church and supported his family with a small farm there.

During Pontiac's War the mission records show that Gottleib visited Province Island south of Philadelphia, on October 14, 1763, while the Christian Indians were sent there for protection from irate whites.[74]

Gottlieb died at Shoeneck October 5, 1776 shortly after the outbreak of the Revolution and was survived by his wife Eva and five children. He left a Will which stated, "my dear wife shall have the use and income of my small estate, both real and personal, so long that she lives for to sustain her in food and apparel". Upon her death the estate was to be divided among his five children Anna Maria, Joseph, Gottlieb, Christoph, and Rosina.[75] The inventory of his estate referred to 21 acres where he lived and 12 ½ additional acres on the plains. In addition to a cow and heifer, the inventory lists an iron stove, one large and four small brass kettles, a cupboard, 3 pewter basins, 1 dish, 6 plates and spoons, a cupbard and baking trough, a pepper mill and coffee pot, barrel, tubs, pails, a grubbing hoe, spade, iron wedges, maw, ax shovel, weeding hoe, drawing knife, scythe, wool cards, wheel barrow, 2 hives

---

[72] *Pennsylvania Archives* 3rd Ser. Vol 26, p. 60.

[73] *Pennsylvania Archives* 3rd Ser. Vol 26, p. 61.

[74] Rev. Carl John Fliegel, *Index to Records of the Moravian Mission Among the Indians of North America* Vol 2, 1970, reference to B 124, p. 4.

[75] Register of Wills, Northampton County, Pa., Case no 694.

with bees.[76] Gottleib's wife Eva died August 20, 1784. They are both buried at the cemetery of the Moravian Church at Shoeneck.

The children of Gottleib and Eva mentioned in the Will were Anna Marie, born September 5, 1746, Joseph born December 1, 1748, Gottleib Jr. born Nov. 18, 1750, Christoph born August 22, 1755, and Rosina born after 1756. Anna Marie married Johann Christian Hasse at Bethlehem on October 30, 1790.[77] Joseph, Gottleib Jr. and Christoph all owned land and raised families in the vicinity of Shoeneck and Nazareth.[78] Christoph and Gottleib both moved to the Moravian settlement at Gnadenhutten, Tuscarawas County, Ohio

The President is descended from Gottlieb's son Christoph who was born at Allemangel in 1755, the year the attacks by hostile Indians forced the residents of the area to flee for protection to Nazareth and Bethlehem. During the Revolutionary War Christoph and his brother Gottlieb served in the militia under Captain Jacob Heller.[79] In September 1800 Christoph and his son visited the new village at Gnadenhutten and the mission at Goshen on the Muskingum in Ohio.[80] During the next four years his son John drove a

---

[76] Register of Wills, Northampton, Pa., Case no. 694

[77] Marriage Register, Bethlehem Moravian Church, p. 112.

[78] *Pennsylvania Archives* 3rd Ser. Vol 26, pp. 62, 63, 65; Vol 19 pp. 265, 380.

[79] *Pennsylvania Archives* 3rd Ser. Vol 26, pp. 62, 63, 65; Vol 19 pp. 265, 380. Their service in the Revolution is commemorated in a monument located at the cemetery in Gnadenhutten, Ohio. On his father's side President Bush is descended from another Revolutionary War veteran, Col. Samuel Herrick of the Vermont Militia. *The SAR Magazine*, winter 2001, vol. XCV, no. 3, p.5.

[80] *Diary of the Moravian Church at Gnadenhutten July 16, 1800 to August 5, 1805* by Kudwif Huebner, pastor, translated by Allen P. Zimmerman, p. 8; Carl John Fliegel, *Index to the Records of the Moravian Mission Among the Indians Vol 2, 1970*. The reference is to B 171, p. 7 of the records.

wagon between Bethlehem and Gnadenhutten and Goshen, a distance of 400 miles across the mountains, and between Gnadenhutten and Georgetown on the Ohio River, bringing mail, goods for the store, church leaders and new settlers. The following entries from the Gnadenhutten Diary show his role with the new settlement:

October 31, 1801 The young Demuth from Shoeneck came and informed us that his wagon with store goods was on the road between here and Georgetown. Since one of the horses became lame, he had ridden here to procure an extra team.

November 2, 1801 John Demuth, drayman, Bethlehem, arrived at Gnadenhutten with mail.

November 13, 1801 John Demuth to take mail back to Bethlehem.

May 22, 1802 Demuth's wagon from Bethlehem arrived here with merchandise for the store so that to our joy we received many letters and information from there.

May 23, 1802 John Demuth visitor at Goshen

May 31, 1802 John Demuth took letters and diaries for Bethlehem.

June 2, 1802 Demuth's wagon arrived from Georgetown with the balance of the merchandise.

November 20, 1802 Brother Heckewelder came back from Bethlehem and soon thereafter Demuth's wagon arrived here from there. By this means we received letters from the Pennsylvania churches.

November 22, 1802 Demuth's wagon again returned to Bethlehem.

November 23, 1802 John Demuth regular trip between Gnadenhutten and Bethlehem.

September 24, 1803 John Demuth's wagon drove toward Pittsburgh to get our Brother and Sister Leskiel.

October 8, 1803 John Demuth furnished wagon for Mary Magdalene Leskiel and company.

October 24, 1803 John Demuth took conference visitors to Gnadenhutten.

October 30, 1803 John Demuth's wagon returned to us from Pittsburgh.

April 20, 1804 Demuth's wagon left for Lebanon to bring Uhrich's family out of that vicinity into this neighborhood. We sent letters and our diary to Bethlehem.[81]

Christoph, his wife Susanna and eight daughters arrived at Gnadenhutten July 5, 1803, the year Ohio became a State.[82] They were among the Moravians that the Church

---

[81] *Diary of the Moravian Church at Gnadenhutten July 16, 1800 to August 5, 1805* by Kudwif Huebner, pastor, translated by Allen P. Zimmerman; Carl John Fliegel, *Index to the Records of the Moravian Mission Among the Indians Vol 2, 1970*, references to John Demuth at the Goshen Mission.
[82] *Diary of the Moravian Church at Gnadenhutten July 16, 1800 to August 5, 1805* by Kudwif Huebner, pastor, translated by Allen P. Zimmerman p.

persuaded to come to Gnadenhutten to support the mission at Goshen. They settled on land near Gnadenhutten and later that year moved from the farm into the village. By the end of that year the Moravian congregation there had grown to 139, an increase of 50 over the prior year.[83]

In order to appreciate their decision to come west to the Ohio wilderness, it is helpful to understand what it was like at the Moravian communities of Bethlehem, Nazareth, and Shoeneck where they came from. John C. Ogden visited the Moravian communities in 1799 and wrote a book on what he saw.[84] He was impressed by the affable manners of everyone he met. He was impressed by how organized the communities were, the flowers, and the music. Even though life revolved around the church, the church buildings were not ostentatious and the ministers were not pompous or ostentatious. In fact they were meek-mannered and affable. Profits from the church owned enterprises went for missionary work. The sick, old and poor were all taken care of by the community. He was taken to Shoeneck about a mile from Nazareth and said, "The village consists of farmers and tradesmen who reside near a chapel and congregation-house." He visited two of the large church-owned farms near Nazareth which were well-tended and productive. He stated, "The whole country around Nazareth is fertile and presents entertaining objects to the eye."

In contrast Gnadenhutten, Ohio in 1803 was still little more than a clearing in the wilderness. The village consisted of church and general store and a few houses. A family

---

91; Gnadenhutten Moravian Church death records of Christoph Demuth and Susannah Demuth state their date of arrival.

[83] *Diary of the Moravian Church at Gnadenhutten July 16, 1800 to August 5, 1805* by Kudwif Huebner, pastor, translated by Allen P. Zimmerman p. 92.

[84] John C. Ogden, *An Excursion into Bethelehm and Nazareth in Pennsylvania in the Year 1799*, Philadelphia, 1805.

arriving from the east faced the task of locating their piece of the woods, constructing a cabin, and clearing some land for a corn and vegetable patch. Christoph was 48 years old when he arrived in the wilderness. He was the head of a household that included a wife and eight daughters. His only son had already started his own family and was still driving a wagon between Gnadenhutten and Bethlehem.

The church was obviously a big part of the Demuths life, and they were active in the congregation at Gnadenhutten. On December 26, 1803, daughter Rachel, age 15, "was received into the congregation and commended to the Savior's blessing in prayer on our knees." On March 29, 1804, daughter Rosina, age 20, was in attendance as a candidate. Daughter Ann Maria, age 19, was "received into the single sister's choir with the laying on of hands" on May 4, 1804. Her sister Rachel was received into the choir of unmarried sisters on May 4, 1805. Daughter Margaret was taken into the older girls choir on June 4, 1805.[85]

Christoph received a deed for 175 acres for a tract that extended on both sides of the Muskingum (now Tuscarawas) River. The deed was from Abraham Levering of Lititz, Lancaster County, Pennsylvania, and was dated October 4, 1809. The deed recites that Levering acquired the tract from John Heckewelder by deed dated January 12, 1801, and that it was part of the land received by Heckewelder by patent from President John Adams on March 28, 1800. The date of Christoph's deed suggests that he was leasing or purchasing the land by installment payments before he received the deed.

The daughters brought to the frontier by Christoph and Susanna Demuth no doubt attracted considerable interest by the young men of the neighborhood. The family rapidly expanded. Susanna married John Fenner on January 5, 1806.

---

[85] *Diary of the Moravian Church at Gnadenhutten July 16, 1800 to August 5, 1805* by Kudwif Huebner, pastor, translated by Allen P. Zimmerman pp. 87, 98, 101, 118, 128.

On April 2, 1806, Rosanna married Joseph Shamel who had come to the area with his brother George from Wachovia, the Moravian settlement in North Carolina.[86] Anne Marie married Jacob Uhrich at the home of her parents on January 17, 1809.[87] Sarah Catherine married her sister's brother-in-law George Shamel at the Demuth home on December 18, 1810. Margaret married John Flickinger on April 17, 1812, and moved with him to Sandy Creek in the northern part of the County.[88] Abigail married John Niegeman, Lydia married Benjamin Casey, and Rachel married Richard Ferguson.

The year end report for 1812 stated that the Gnadenhutten congregation included 34 families. This included Christoph and Susannah and their daughters and sons-in-law Joseph and Anna Rosina Shamel, George and Sarah Catherine Shamel, Jacob and Anna Marie Uhrich, all living east of Gnadenhutten, and son John living on the west side of the river.[89] Five of the 34 families belonging to the congregation were Demuths.

The church records show the large family was kept busy attending births and baptisms. On December 4, 1811, newborn children of daughters Rosanna, Sarah, Catherine and Rachel were baptized at the home of Christoph and Susanna.[90] A number of baptisms were recorded in the church book of the Moravian congregation at Beersheba, which was located across the river from Gnadenhutten. They show grandparents,

---

[86] Susanna's and Rosanna's marriages are found in Muskingum County Marriage Records 1804-1818 because they took place before Tuscarawas County was organized.

[87] Tuscarawas County Marriage Records 5-73

[88] The marriages of Anna Marie, Sarah Catherine, and Margaret appear in *Diary of Gnadenhutten Congregation 1805-1814* pp. 26, 31, 40.

[89] *Diary of Gnadenhutten Congregation 1805-1814* p. 49, 50.

[90] *Diary of Gnadenhutten Congregation 1805-1814* p. 38.

aunts and uncles frequently served as "sponsors" at the baptisms.[91]

Susanna Catherine Demuth died quickly and unexpectedly on July 15, 1817, due to a severe hemorrhage. She was buried at God's acre at Gnadenhutten. The church diary reported that the church could not hold all those in attendance at her funeral.[92] The death notice that appears in the Church Book reported that she had ten children, 2 sons and 8 daughters and 32 grandchildren. One of her sons predeceased her.[93]

On April 16, 1818, the widower Christoph Demuth married Elizabeth Guenther, widow of Peter Guenther.[94] Peter and Elizabeth had arrived at Gnadenhutten with their four children on November 7, 1802. Peter appears on the memorial in the Gnadenhutten Cemetery honoring veterans of the Revolutionary War along with Christoph and his brother Gottleib. Christoph died January 27, 1823, at the age of 67, survived by one son, seven daughters, and 40 grandchildren.[95] The survivors included Margaret Demuth Flickinger, the 4th great grandmother of Barbara Pierce Bush, the mother of President George W. Bush. [96]

By the time of Christoph's death the mission at Goshen had run its course. Gnadenhutten was no longer a Moravian

---

[91] *Church Book of the Brethren's Congregation at Beersheba* translated by Maxine Renner Eberle, 1987, pp. 25-27.

[92] *Diary of Gnadenhutten, Beersheba, and Sharon May 1, 1816 to Dec 31, 1826*, translated by Allen P. Zimmerman, 1955, p. 19.

[93] Death Register, Gnadenhutten Moravian Church, p. 297.

[94] *Diary of Gnadenhutten, Beersheba, and Sharon May 1, 1816 to Dec 31, 1826*, translated by Allen P. Zimmerman, 1955, p. 31.

[95] Death Register, Gnadenhutten Moravian Church p. 300.

[96] For the descent of George W. Bush from Christoph's daughter Margaret Demuth see the Appendix and for more detail see Thomas Stephen Neel and Sandra Anderson Peters, "The Ohio Ancestors of Past President George H. W. Bush and Former First Lady Barbara Pierce Bush", *The Report*, Ohio Genealogical Society, Vol. 40, Number 2 pp. 71-92

town, which existed to support a mission. It was one of many villages on the Ohio frontier where people of diverse backgrounds were hard at work converting a wilderness into productive farms. Out of their diversity and common experience emerged a hope of what America could become, a land where the extraordinary hopes of ordinary people could be realized, a land where people are entitled to be treated with respect regardless of their wealth, ancestry, race, gender or religion, a land where hard work and ingenuity are admired and where those in need are treated with compassion and dignity. Living on the Ohio frontier among people of diverse backgrounds and faiths and sharing with them the challenge of the frontier, the Demuth family grew out of and out grew the Moravian culture, which had shaped the first few generations of the family in America. The inspiration that motivated the Demuths and other Moravians to come to America and work to create a more compassionate world became part of the many contributions, which shaped the American dream. By going back to the original sources of that dream, we not only honor those who created it, but we keep it alive so that it may continue to inspire the faith, hope, and commitment of millions of Americans and millions of ordinary people outside America who look to America as the best hope for the ordinary man and woman.

CHAPTER EIGHT

FROM WIDOW WITH SIX SMALL CHILDREN

TO FIRST LADY

The final chapter of this book will trace the history of the family from the Moravians Christoph and Susanna Catherine Demuth to the President's mother, Barbara Bush. Although Barbara was born in New York, this is primarily a story about Ohio families, which spans much of the history of the State. Although the generations after the Demuths were not members of the Moravian Church, the Christian faith remained an important part of their lives. There were hard times in the lives of these families, which tested their faith, hard times which they overcame with strength, hope and compassion for the suffering of others.

Christoph and Susanna Catherine Demuth's daughter Margaret married John Flickinger on April 7, 1812, at the home of her parents.[97] John, a farmer residing on Sandy Creek in the northeast corner of Tuscarawas County, was born September 18, 1787, in Frederick County, Maryland. His religion was Reformed, which suggests a Swiss, German or Dutch ancestry. He was the son of Michael and Mary

---

[97] Tuscarawas County, Ohio Marriage Records Vol. 1, page 10, Return 73. They were married by Moravian Minister George G. Muller.

Flickinger who moved to Tuscarawas County in 1807.[98] His father was a well-to-do farmer who purchased 480 acres from the government in Sandy Township.[99] This land was raw wilderness when it was purchased from the government and required considerable work to convert to productive farm land.

Shortly after John and Margaret were married, the War of 1812 erupted, which in the Ohio country brought fears of Indian attacks. John served in the militia unit of his brother-in-law George Shamel during the War of 1812.[100]

Although Mr. Flickinger was not a member of the congregation, the records of the Moravian Church at Gnadenhutten and Beersheba, located across the river from Gnadenhutten, show the baptisms of their first four children. Their first child was Ann Maria, born March 14, 1813, and baptized on May 16 by Rev. Muller at the home of Margaret's sister Rachel Ferguson.[101] Son Christoph was born May 7, 1814, and baptized on August 10. Margaret's parents were

---

[98] Church Book of Gnadenhutten Moravian Church, Marriage Register, p. 221; *History of Tuscarawas County, Ohio*, Warner Beers & Co., 1884, p. 645. Robert Elliott Flickinger, *The Flickinger Family History*, Des Moines, Iowa: Success Composition and Printing Co., p. 103. The Flickinger Family History erroneously states that they came from Germany and settled in the county in 1818. The Marriage Register refers to John's mother as "Barbara". In subsequent deed records she signed her name as Mary. John's brother Jacob's wife's name was Barbara which may have caused the mistake in the Church record.

[99] Tuscarawas County, Ohio Deed Book 3, pages 17, 18. The patents were dated in 1812, 1814, and 1816. Since patents were not issued until all payments were made, the land may have been purchased several years earlier.

[100] *Roster of Ohio Soldiers in the War of 1812*, Adjutant General of Ohio, Heritage Books, 1995, p. 138.

[101] Church Book of Gnadenhutten Moravian Church, Baptismal Register p. 21.

listed as the child's sponsors.[102] As an adult this son was known as Christian, lived in Gnadenhutten, and was a member of the Moravian congregation there. He died of typhoid fever when he was only 28, leaving a grieving widow and young children.[103] Their next son Levi was born August 11, 1815, and baptized by the Moravian minister on November 14, 1815.[104] Later in life he moved to Union County with his younger brother Stephen. John Jr. was born October 9, 1817, and was baptized on Christmas Day.[105] He died young, as did his two sisters. A son Eli was born February 16, 1820. In 1863 he moved to Iowa.[106] The youngest son Stephen was born May 4, 1823, and baptized June 4, 1823 by Rev. Josiah Foster, the pastor of the Lutheran Church in Sandy Township. The baptism certificate was passed down in the family to Barbara Bush's grandmother.[107]

Tragedy struck the year following Stephen's birth. On November 4, 1824, John Flickinger died at the age of 37, and on November 6 the Moravian minister arrived at the Flickinger's home in Sandyville to conduct John's funeral. The minister commented in his diary, "A goodly number of attentive hearers were present." The minister who preached the next day, a Sunday, at the school house in Sandyville

---

[102] Maxine Renner Eberlis, translator, *Church Book of the Brethren's Congregation at Beersheba*, Ragersville Historical Society, 1987, baptism of children not belonging to the Society #44

[103] Church Book of Gnadenhutten Moravian Church, Death Register, p. 323.

[104] Maxine Renner Eberlis, translator, *Church Book of the Brethren's Congregation at Beersheba*, Ragersville Historical Society, 198, baptism of children not belonging to the Society #51

[105] Maxine Renner Eberlis, translator, *Church Book of the Brethren's Congregation at Beersheba*, Ragersville Historical Society, 1987, baptism of children not belonging to the Society #79.

[106] Robert Elliott Flickinger, *The Flickinger Family History*, Des Moines, Iowa: Success Composition and Printing Co. p. 106.

[107] Robert Elliott Flickinger, *The Flickinger Family History*, Des Moines, Iowa: Success Composition and Printing Co. p. 109.

commented in his diary, "as it was very cold and the schoolhouse was without windows and doors only a few people were present."[108] Margaret who was left alone with six children ranging from age one to ten must have indeed felt a chill gripping her heart.

Although it is difficult to imagine today, the frontier was a very dangerous place to live because of disease, which attacked the settlers. In both 1823 and 1824 the diaries of the Moravian ministers refer to the many deaths as a result of "the fever." One of the Moravian ministers stated in his diary, "We were completely occupied with visiting the sick between the funerals."[109] He also stated, "It is very gratifying that most of the sick are quite resigned to the will of the Saviour. May this time of testing bring about serious reflection, that we, by word and deed may become more pleasing to our crucified Saviour and that his divine peace may live in our souls."[110]

Margaret's brother John served as administrator of her husband's estate, and her brothers-in-law Jacob Uhrich and Joseph Shamel signed his bond.[111] There is no record of John owning real estate, so it is likely that they were living on the land of his father Michael. Although he may have compensated Margaret for the improvements made by John to his land, there is no indication in the county records that John's farm was conveyed to Margaret or her children, or that John's children inherited anything from their grandfather's estate.[112]

---

[108] Moravian Diaries of the Ministers of the Gnadenhutten Moravian Church, Part III, p. 130, 131.

[109] Moravian Diaries of the Ministers of the Gnadenhutten Moravian Church, Part III, p. 111.

[110] Moravian Diaries of the Ministers of the Gnadenhutten Moravian Church, Part III, p. 113.

[111] Tuscarawas County Probate Court, Administration Docket No. 1, 2, and 3, p. 29.

[112] Tuscarawas County Probate Court, Administration Docket 1,2,1, p. 245; Account Book 3, p. 296, Account Book 5, p. 112; Chancery Record Book

A little over a year after John's death, on January 8, 1826, Margaret and James Tracy were married by Rev. Jacob Rauschenberger, the Moravian minister at Gnadenhutten, in her house at Sandy Creek.[113] James, born Dec. 17, 1799, was the oldest son of James and Elizabeth Tracy, Methodists from Virginia, who were among the early settlers of the Gnadenhutten area. The Tracys rented a farm from a Moravian near Gnadenhutten. James was six years younger than Margaret. He had lost his mother and sister to illness in 1823.[114]

The couple farmed Margaret's place for a while, but by 1830 they were living in Rush Township south of Uhrichsville.[115] In 1833 James purchased a farm south of Uhrichsville near the village of Newport for $2,000.[116] James and his family were among the early members of the Methodist church at Newport.[117] The Tracys had a house filled not only with John and Margaret's children, but also several children of James and Margaret. In 1840 there were still seven children in the home.[118] By 1850, Margaret had died and three of James and Margaret's children aged 20, 18, and 15 were living with their father.[119] James died May 24, 1889.[120]

Margaret and John's youngest son Stephen grew up on James and Margaret's farm and was educated in the district

3, p. 493- 499. Deed records show that the real estate which was not sold to third parties was transferred to Michael's sons Jacob and Peter.

[113] Tuscarawas County Marriage Records Vols. 1,2 and 3, p. 100, Return 793.

[114] *Moravian Diaries of the Ministers of the Gnadenhutten Moravian Church*, Part III, p. 111, 113.

[115] 1830 Census Tuscarawas County, Rush Township, p. 032.

[116] Tuscarawas County, Ohio Deed Book 19, p. 708.

[117] *History of Tuscarawas County, Ohio*, Warner Beers & Co., 1884, p. 583.

[118] 1840 Census Tuscarawas County, p. 328.

[119] 1850 Census Tuscarawas County, Mill Township, p. 302

[120] *Tuscarawas County Cemeteries* Vol. V, Newport Cemetery.

school.[121]   He married Margaret A. Figley August 7, 1845, in Tuscarawas County.[122] In 1848 he purchased 101 acres near Uhrichsville for $433.[123] In 1853 he sold the farm for $1,000.[124] The family then moved to York Township, Union County, Ohio.[125] His older brother Levi sold his real estate in and adjacent to Uhrichsville, formerly known as Trenton, and also moved his family to Union County.[126]

Stephen died January 22, 1869, at only 45 years of age, leaving a widow and large family of children.[127] The county history described Stephen as follows, "He was an exemplary man in life, modest in manner, charitable in all things and highly esteemed throughout the community. For many years he was a member of the Methodist Episcopal Church, taking an active interest in his church duties and leading a true Christian life."[128] His widow Margaret died July 30, 1886, and is buried in the York Center Cemetery beside her husband.[129] The children of Stephen and Margaret were William, Jacob, Eliza, Margaret, John, Joseph and Mary.[130]

---

[121] *History of Union County, Ohio*, Warner Beers & Co., 1883, p. 542.
[122] Tuscarawas County Marriage Records Vol 4 & 5, p. 24, Return 4329; Church Book of the Gnadenhutten Moravian Church, Marriage Register p. 231.
[123] Tuscarawas County Deed Book 26, p. 296.
[124] Tuscarawas County Deed Book 37, p. 449.
[125] *History of Union County, Ohio*, Warner Beers & Co., 1883, p. 541, 542.
[126] Tuscarawas County Deed Book 40, p. 63. When the deed was signed on December 12, 1854, Levi and his wife were already residing in Union County.
[127] York Township, Union Co., Ohio Cemeteries, Union Co. Genealogical Society, p. 29.

[128] *History of Union County, Ohio*, Warner Beers & Co., 1883, p. 541, 542
[129] York Township, Union Co., Ohio Cemeteries, Union Co. Genealogical Society, p. 29.
[130] Robert Elliott Flickinger, *The Flickinger Family History*, Des Moines, Iowa: Success Composition and Printing Co. p. 110.

Stephen's son Jacob Martin Flickinger, born in 1849, married Sarah A. Haines on June 13, 1872.[131] Sarah was born in 1855, the daughter of Jonathan and Mary Haines. Jonathan's father was one of the first settlers of Washington Township, Union County, Ohio, and platted the village of Hainesville in 1838.[132] Jonathan was one of the first settlers of Champaign County, Ohio.[133] Mary's brother William served in the First Battalion Ohio Sharpshooters in the Army of the Cumberland. He was taken prisoner on November 8, 1864, and confined in nine different Confederate prisons before he was released at the end of the War. In addition to farming, he served as a local minister of the Methodist Episcopal Church.[134] Jacob Martin Flickinger was a farmer near Byhalia, the only village in Washington Township, Union County, and for a time owned the hotel there.[135] Martin and his wife Sarah had only one child Lulu Dell Flickinger, who was born in 1876. Sarah died March 25, 1888, at the age of 33, when her daughter was only 12 years old.[136] On March 28, 1889, Martin married Rosa Tropp.[137]

Lula Dell Flickinger graduated from Richwood High School and married James Edgar Robinson on March 31, 1895.[138] James, was born August 15, 1868, in Paris Township, Union County, the son of John W. Robinson (1831-1920) and Sarah Coe Robinson (1831-1901).[139] The Robinsons were

---

[131] Union County Marriage Record Book C, p. 29.

[132] *History of Union County, Ohio*, Warner Beers & Co., 1883, p. 660, 662.

[133] *History of Union County, Ohio*, Warner Beers & Co., 1883, p. 937.

[134] *History of Union County, Ohio*, Warner Beers & Co., 1883, p. 668, 669.

[135] *History of Union County, Ohio*, Warner Beers & Co., 1883, p. 664.

[136] York Township, Union Co., Ohio Cemeteries, Union Co. Genealogical Society, p. 29.

[137] Union County Marriage Record Book E, p. 9.

[138] Marion Co. Marriage Record Book Vol. 11.

[139] Memorial 124 *Ohio State Reports* lxxiii; Oakdale Cemetery, Marysville, Union County, Ohio, Union County Chapter of the Ohio Genealogical Society, p. 124.

early settlers of Ohio. John's grandfather, Rev. James Robinson, was a Presbyterian minister who came to Pickaway County, Ohio, to accept the pastorate of two churches. His son John Sr. married Elizabeth Mitchell and settled on a farm in Union County. John was an elder of the Presbyterian Church, a Justice of the Peace and County Commissioner. The couple had ten children including John Jr., James E. Robinson's father.[140]

After graduating from Marysville High School, James E. Robinson spent two years at Ohio Wesleyan in Delaware, Ohio, and then a year at Ohio State University. He spent a year in the office of his uncle reading law and then went back to Ohio State University to study at its new law school. He was admitted to the bar in 1893, and for the next six years practiced law at Richwood, Ohio. He was elected County Prosecutor of Union County for two terms during which time the family lived in Marysville, Ohio. Following several years in private practice in Marysville, James was appointed by the Governor as a state appellate judge in his district. In 1918 he was elected to the Ohio Supreme Court and reelected in 1924 and 1930. Following his election to the Ohio Supreme Court, the family moved to Columbus, Ohio.[141] James and Lulu had four children, Pauline, Sarah, Eloise, and James. Following the tradition of the Robinson family, James and Lulu were members of the Presbyterian Church.

The father died January 27, 1932, survived by Lulu and the four children.[142] He suffered a stroke at age 63, which

---

[140] *History of Union County*, Ohio, Vol II, W.H. Beers & Co., 1883, p. 227, 228.

[141] Robert Elliott Flickinger, *The Flickinger Family History*, Des Moines, Iowa: Success Composition and Printing Co. p. 110; W.L. Curry, *History of Union County, Ohio*, Indianapolis: B.F. Bowen & Co. 1915, p. 604. A photograph of Mr. Robinson appears with his biography; Memorial 124 *Ohio State Reports* lxxiii; *Columbus Dispatch*, January 27, 1932, p. 1.

[142] Memorial 124 *Ohio State Reports* lxxiii; *Columbus Dispatch*, January 27, 1932, p. 1; Ohio Death Certificate, Vol. 6803, certificate #2307.

brought a sudden end to a spectacular career. He was a popular and highly respected jurist.[143] Judge Mathias with whom he had served for a number of years, stated, "In the death of Judge Robinson, the citizens of Ohio have sustained a severe loss. He was a high-minded, impartial and conscientious Judge ... He had sincere convictions and not only the ability, but the courage to state them. He had the confidence of those with whom he worked and was by them held in high esteem."[144]

In her Memoir, Barbara Bush, stated that after her husband's death, her grandmother changed. Before his death, like most women of her day, she was devoted to taking care of her home and husband. She taught herself to drive following his death and with several friends traveled around the United States, Canada and Mexico in a car pulling a small trailer.[145] Mrs. Robinson was Barbara's best-loved grandparent.[146] She died in 1957.[147]

James and Lulu's daughter Pauline graduated from Marysville High School and then Miami University at Oxford, Ohio, where she met Marvin Pierce, a star athlete and scholar. They were married in 1918. The Pierces eventually moved to Rye, New York. Marvin commuted to New York City where he worked for McCall's Publishing Company. He eventually

---

[143] Memorial 124 *Ohio State Reports* lxxiii; *Columbus Dispatch*, January 27, 1932, p. 1; Editorial, *Columbus Dispatch*, January 28, 1932.

[144] Memorial 124 *Ohio State Reports* lxxiii; *Columbus Dispatch*, January 27, 1932.

[145] Barbara Bush, *A Memoir*; New York: Charles Scribner's Sons, 1994, p. 9.

[146] Barbara Bush, *A Memoir*; New York: Charles Scribner's Sons, 1994, p. 9.

[147] Oakdale Cemetery, Marysville, Union County, Ohio, Vol 1, Union County Chapter of the Ohio Gealogical Society, p. 174.

became president and then chairman of the board of the company.[148] Barbara was born in 1925 at Rye.

Barbara married George Herbert Walker Bush in Rye, New York, in 1945. Their first child George Walker Bush was born July 6, 1946. At the time of his birth, the couple was living at New Haven, Connecticut, while George attended Yale University. Barbara's mother Pauline died in an automobile accident in 1949, while Barbara was pregnant with their second child.[149] The child was named Pauline Robinson Bush after her recently deceased grandmother. Robin, as she was called, died of leukemia when she was three. Barbara stated in her Memoir that when she held her dying little girl, she never felt God's presence more strongly.[150]

In every generation from the Moravian Demuths to Barbara Bush, an untimely death tested the faith of family members. John Flickinger died at age 37 leaving Margaret a widow with six children aged one to ten. Their son Stephen died at age 45 leaving Margaret a widow with a large family. Their son Martin married Sarah Haines who died at age 33 when their daughter Lulu was twelve. Lulu's husband James Robinson died at age 63 while a sitting judge on the Ohio Supreme Court at the height of his career. Their daughter Pauline Robinson Pierce died in an automobile accident. Her daughter Barbara and husband George H. W. Bush lost their daughter Robin when she was only three years old. This is a family, which for generations responded to suffering with strength, hope and compassion for the suffering of others.

---

[148] *The Report*, The Ohio Genealogical Society, Vol. 40, Number 2, Summer 2000, p. 76; *Who Was Who In America* Vol. V 1969-1973, p. 570.

[149] Barbara Bush, *A Memoir*; New York: Charles Scribner's Sons, 1994, p. 36.

[150] Barbara Bush, *A Memoir*; New York: Charles Scribner's Sons, 1994, p. 44

APPENDIX

ANCESTORS OF GEORGE W. BUSH

Generation No. 1

1. George Walker Bush, born July 6, 1946. He was the son of **2. George Herbert Walker Bush** and **3. Barbara Pierce**. He married **(1) Laura Welch** 1977. She was born in Midland, Texas.

Generation No. 2

2. George Herbert Walker Bush, born June 12, 1924 in Milton, Norfolk Co., MA. He married **3. Barbara Pierce** January 6, 1945 in Rye, New York. 41st President of the United States 1989-1993.

3. Barbara Pierce, born June 8, 1925 in Rye, New York. She was the daughter of **6. Marvin Pierce** and **7. Pauline Robinson**.

Generation No. 3

6. Marvin Pierce, born June 17, 1893 in Sharpsville, Pa., died July 17, 1969. He married **7. Pauline Robinson** August 1918. He was president of McCall's Publishing Co.

7. Pauline Robinson, born 1896; died September 23, 1949. She was the daughter of **14. James Edgar Robinson** and **15. Lulu Dell Flickinger**.

Generation No. 4

14. James Edgar Robinson, born August 15, 1868 in Union Co., Ohio; died January 26, 1932. He married **15. Lulu Dell Flickinger** May 31, 1893 in Marion Co., Ohio. He was Justice of Ohio Supreme Court 1919-1932.

15. Lulu Dell Flickinger, born 1876 in Union Co., Ohio, died 1957. She was the daughter of **30. Jacob Marion Flickinger** and **31. Sarah A. Haines**.

Generation No. 5

30. Jacob Marion Flickinger, born 1849 in Tuscarawas County, Ohio; died January 20, 1917 in Morrow Co., Ohio. He was the son of **60. Stephen Flickinger** and **61. Margaret Anne Figley**. He married **31. Sarah A. Haines** June 13, 1872 in Union Co., Ohio.

31. Sarah A. Haines, born 1855; died March 25, 1888 in Union Co., Ohio.

Generation No. 6

60. Stephen Flickinger, born May 4, 1823 in Tuscarawas County, Ohio; died January 22, 1869 in Union Co., Ohio. He was the son of **120. John Flickinger** and **121. Margaret Demuth**. He married **61. Margaret Anne Figley** August 7, 1845 in Tuscarawas County, Ohio.

61. Margaret Anne Figley, born December 23, 1825 in

144

Tuscarawas County, Ohio; died July 30, 1886 in Union Co.,
Ohio.

120. John Flickinger, born September 18, 1787 in
Frederick Co., Md., died November 4, 1824 at Sandyville,
Ohio. He married **121. Margaret Demuth** April 7, 1812 in
Tuscarawas County, Ohio.

121. Margaret Demuth, born March 10, 1793 in
Northampton Co., Pa., died bef. 1850 in Tuscarawas Co.,
Ohio. She was the daughter of **242. Christopher Demuth**
and **243. Susanna Catherine Klein**.

Children of John Flickinger and Margaret Demuth are:

  i.   Christopher Flickinger, born May 7, 1814 at Sandyville, Ohio,
       died September 28, 1842 at Gnadenhutten, Ohio
 ii.   Levi Flickinger, born August 11, 1815 in Tuscarawas County,
       Ohio, died in Union Co., Ohio.
 iii. John Flickinger, born October 9, 1817
60 iv. Stephen Flickinger, born May 4, 1823 in Tuscarawas County,
       Ohio; died January 22, 1869 in Union Co., Ohio; married
       Margaret Anne Figley August 7, 1845 in Tuscarawas County,
       Ohio.

242. Christopher Demuth, born August 22, 1755 in
Allemangel, Pa; died January 27, 1823 in Warwick Twp.,
Tuscarawas Co., Oh. He was the son of **484. Gottleib
Demuth** and **485. Eva Barbira Gutsler**. He married **243.
Susanna Catherine Klein** April 8, 1777 in Shoeneck, Pa.
Moved from Shoeneck, Pa. to Gnadenhutten, Ohio in 1803.

243. Susanna Catherine Klein, born January 2, 1758 in
Northampton Co., Pa.; died July 15, 1817 in Warwick, Twp.,
Tuscarawas Co., Oh. She was the daughter of **486. Andreas**

Henry Klein and **487. Jane Elizabeth Thomas**.

Generation No. 9

484. Gottleib Demuth, born October 10, 1715 in
Schonau, Moravia; died October 5, 1776 in Shoeneck, Pa. He
was the son of **968. Tobias Demuth** and **969. Rosina Tonn**.
He married **485. Eva Barbira Gutsler** Abt. 1739. Moved to
Herrnhut in 1727. Among first group of Missionaries to
Savanah, Georgia in 1735. Moved to Germantown,
Pennsylvania in 1738. Assisted with construction of first
buildings at Bethlehem in 1741 and 1741.

485. Eva Barbira Gutsler, born November 11, 1713 in
Hilsheim, Palatinate; died August 20, 1784 in Shoeneck, Pa.;
She was the daughter of **970. Heinrich Gutsler** and **971.
Anna Marie ?.**

486. Andreas Henry Klein, born October 4, 1733 in
Zweibrucken; died January 7, 1786 in Northampton Co., Pa.
He married **487. Jane Elizabeth Thomas**.

487. Jane Elizabeth Thomas, born March 5, 1733/34 in
Pa.; died August 20, 1820 in Shoeneck, Northampton Co., Pa.

Generation No. 10

968. Tobias Demuth, born 1680 in Karlsdorf, Moravia;
died 1715 in Moravia. He was the son of **1936. Christoph
Demuth** and **1937. Elizabeth**. He married **969. Rosina Tonn**
in Moravia.

969. Rosina Tonn, born 1682 in Moravia; died
September 27, 1732 in Herrnhut, Saxony.

146

970. Heinrich Gutsler He married **971. Anna Marie ?**.
971. Anna Marie ?

Generation No. 11

1936. Christoph Demuth, born Abt. 1655 in Moravia; died 1727 in Moravia. He married **1937. Elizabeth ?**[151]

---

[151] Documentation for this Ancestor Tree of George W. Bush has been personally researched by the author and is found in the footnotes in Chapters 7 and 8. This ancestor tree follows only the line of the President to his Moravian ancestors, which is the subject of this book. For those interested in other Ohio ancestral lines of the President on both his father and mother's side, see Thomas Stephen Neel and Sundra Anderson Peters, "The Ohio Ancestors of Past President George H. W. Bush and Former First Lady Barbara Pierce Bush," *The Report*, The Ohio Genealogical Society, Vol. 40, Number 2, Summer 2000, p. 71.

APPENDIX

DESCENDANTS

OF

CHRISTOPH AND ELIZABETH DEMUTH

Generation No. 1

1. CHRISTOPH[1] DEMUTH was born abt. 1655 in Karlsdorf, Moravia, and died 1727 in Moravia. He married ELIZABETH ?.

Children of CHRISTOPH DEMUTH and ELIZABETH ? are:
2.   i.   TOBIAS[2] DEMUTH, b. 1680, Karlsdorf, Moravia; d. 1715, Moravia.
       ii. JUSTINA DEMUTH, b. 1683, Moravia; d. November 25, 1732, Herrnhut, Saxony.
3.   iii. GOTTHARD DEMUTH, b. Aft. 1689, Karlsdorf, Moravia; d. December 11, 1744, Germantown, Pa.
4.   iv. JOHANN CHRISTOPH DEMUTH, b. November 9, 1689, Karlsdorf, Moravia; d. March 5, 1754, Nazareth, Pa.
5.   v.   MARIA MAGDALENA DEMUTH, b. 1696.

Generation No. 2

2. TOBIAS[2] DEMUTH *(CHRISTOPH[1])* was born 1680 in Karlsdorf, Moravia, and died 1715 in Moravia. He married ROSINA TONN 1704 in Moravia. She was born 1682 in Moravia, and died September 27, 1732 in

Herrnhut, Saxony.

Children of TOBIAS DEMUTH and ROSINA TONN are:

6.   i.   ANNA ROSINA[3] DEMUTH, d. 1745, Herrnhag.
7.   ii.   VERONICA DEMUTH, b. February 4, 1705/06, Karlsdorf, Moravia; d. October 5, 1765, St. Thomas, West Indies.
8.   iii.   JOSEPH DEMUTH, b. March 19, 1706/07, Karlsdorf, Moravia; d. November 27, 1783, Zeist.
9.   iv.   ANNA MARIA DEMUTH, b. November 17, 1712, Karlsdorf, Moravia; d. January 20, 1760, Bethlehem, Pa..
10.   v.   GOTTLEIB DEMUTH, b. October 10, 1715, Schonau, Moravia; d. October 5, 1776, Shoeneck, Pa.

3. GOTTHARD[2] DEMUTH *(CHRISTOPH[1])* was born aft. 1689 in Karlsdorf, Moravia, and died December 11, 1744 in Germantown, Pa. He married REGINA LEOPOLD January 20, 1727/28 in Herrnhut, Saxony, daughter of GEORGE LEOPOLD and ELIZABETH KERN. She was born September 7, 1702 in Weisenstaedtel, Bohemia, and died February 20, 1774 in Bethlehem, Pa.

Children of GOTTHARD DEMUTH and REGINA LEOPOLD are:

      i.   MARIA MAGDALENA[3] DEMUTH, b. May 5, 1729; d. bef. May 8, 1731.
     ii.   JOHANNA ELIZABETH DEMUTH, b. October 1730; d. May 19, 1732.
     iii.   MARIA MAGDALENA DEMUTH, b. May 8, 1731, Herrnhut, Saxony; d. August 8, 1777, Herrnhutt, Saxony.
     iv.   JOHANNES DEMUTH, b. March 26, 1734, Herrnhutt, Saxony; d. June 29, 1737, Herrnhutt, Saxony.
11.   v.   JOHN CHRISTOPHER DEMUTH, b. September 19, 1738, Germantown, Pa; d. September 7, 1818, Lancaster, Pa..
     vi.   CHRISTIAN FREDERICK DEMUTH, b. December 26, 1740, Germantown, Pa; d. September 10, 1781, Hope, NJ; m. MAGDALENA STOTZ, March 14, 1781, Bethlehem, Pa.; b. November 21, 1744, Wurtemberg.

4. JOHANN CHRISTOPH[2] DEMUTH *(CHRISTOPH[1])* was born November 9, 1689 in Karlsdorf, Moravia, and died March 5, 1754 in Nazareth, Pa. He married ANNA MARIA SCHMIDT 1716 in Moravia. She was born November 25, 1697 in Milkendorf, Ober Schlesien, and died February 27, 1761 in Nazareth, Pa.

Children of JOHANN DEMUTH and ANNA SCHMIDT are:

150

12.   i.   REGINA³ DEMUTH, b. November 28, 1716; d. March 6, 1779, Frankebar.
        ii. HANS JOSEPH DEMUTH, b. 1718; d. April 25, 1728, Herrnhut, Saxony.
        iii. ANN DEMUTH, b. 1721; d. October 14, 1728, Herrnhutt, Saxony.
        iv. FERDINAND DEMUTH, b. January 8, 1720/21, Moravia; d. August 30, 1768, Herrnhut, Saxony.
        v.   ANNA DEMUTH, b. April 5, 1731; d. March 14, 1737/38, Herrnhut, Saxony.
        vi. JOHANN MARTIN DEMUTH, b. 1738; d. March 16, 1743/44, Herrnhut, Saxony.

5. MARIA MAGDALENA² DEMUTH *(CHRISTOPH¹)* was born 1696. She married CHRISTIAN WETZEL.

Child of MARIA DEMUTH and CHRISTIAN WETZEL is:
        i.   GOTTFRIED³ WETZEL.

Generation No. 3

6. ANNA ROSINA³ DEMUTH *(TOBIAS², CHRISTOPH¹)* died 1745 in Herrnhag. She married ? HINZ.

Child of ANNA DEMUTH and ? HINZ is:
        i.   PETER⁴ HINZ, d. 1744, Wetterau.

7. VERONICA³ DEMUTH *(TOBIAS², CHRISTOPH¹)* was born February 4, 1705/06 in Karlsdorf, Moravia, and died October 5, 1765 in St. Thomas, West Indies. She married (1) VALENTINE LOEHANS 1738 in St. Thomas, West Indies. He died 1742. She married (2) JOHANN BOEHNER 1743. He died 1785.

Children of VERONICA DEMUTH and JOHANN BOEHNER are:
        i.   BENIGNA⁴ BOEHNER, b. August 17, 1749, St. Thomas, West Indies; d. October 24, 1792, Bethania, North Carolina; m. SIMON C. PETER, July 29, 1784, Lititz, Pennsylvania.
        ii. ELIZABETH BOEHNER, b. October 16, 1751, St. Thomas, West Indies.
        iii. PAUL BOEHNER, b. June 19, 1745, St. Thomas, West Indies; d. January 3, 1747/48, Bethlehem, Pa..

8. JOSEPH[3] DEMUTH *(TOBIAS[2], CHRISTOPH[1])* was born March 19, 1706/07 in Karlsdorf, Moravia, and died November 27, 1783 in Zeist. He married JUDITH SCHAUL November 1738 in Zeist, Germany. She was born September 1, 1710 in Dessau, and died January 30, 1793 in Zeist.

Children of JOSEPH DEMUTH and JUDITH SCHAUL are:
  i. ANNA MARIE[4] DEMUTH, b. July 4, 1741, Zeist; d. January 11, 1798, Zeist.
  ii. DAVID DEMUTH, b. December 16, 1741, Herrnhag; d. December 8, 1777, Gnadenberg.
  iii. JOSEPH DEMUTH, b. March 5, 1743/44, Herrnhag; d. January 8, 1776, Gnadenberg.
  iv. AGNES DEMUTH, b. August 4, 1749, Zeist or Herrnhag; d. January 3, 1832, Bethlehem, Pa; m. GEORGE MATHEW LOESCH, 1795.
  v. MAGDALENA DEMUTH, b. April 18, 1757, Zeist; d. May 9, 1812, Zeist.

9. ANNA MARIA[3] DEMUTH *(TOBIAS[2], CHRISTOPH[1])* was born November 17, 1712 in Karlsdorf, Moravia, and died January 20, 1760 in Bethlehem, Pa.. She married ANDREW ANTON LAWATCH June 14, 1738. He died 1771 in Surinam.

Children of ANNA DEMUTH and ANDREW LAWATCH are:
  i. MARIA MAGDALENA[4] LAWATCH, b. Abt. 1740; d. 1744, Wetterau.
  ii. JOHN LAWATCH, b. Abt. 1740; d. 1748, Knadenberg.
  iii. ANNA MARIA LAWATCH, b. August 6, 1744, Marienborn; d. April 16, 1778, Herrnhut, Saxony.

10. GOTTLEIB[3] DEMUTH *(TOBIAS[2], CHRISTOPH[1])* was born October 10, 1715 in Schonau, Moravia, and died October 5, 1776 in Shoeneck, Pa. He married EVA BARBIRA GUTSLER Abt. 1739, daughter of HEINRICH GUTSLER and ANNA ?. She was born November 11, 1713 in Hilsheim, Palatinate, and died August 20, 1784 in Shoeneck, Pa.

Children of GOTTLEIB DEMUTH and EVA GUTSLER are:
  i. TOBIAS[4] DEMUTH, b. June 2, 1742, Northampton Co., Pa..
  ii. JOHANNES DEMUTH, b. June 25, 1743, Bethlehem, Pa; d. September 14, 1745.
  iii. GOTTLIEB DEMUTH, b. February 1744/45, Bethlehem, Pa; d. October 2, 1746.
  iv. ANNA MARIA DEMUTH, b. September 5, 1746, Frederickstown,

Pa.; d. April 1, 1813, Bethlehem, Pa; m. JOHANN CHRISTIAN
HASSE, October 30, 1790, Bethlehem, Pa; b. 1714; d. 1797.

    v.   JOSEF DEMUTH, b. December 1, 1748, Fredrickstown, Pa; d. 1827;
m. MARIA MAGDALENA SCHNALL, August 15, 1787, Moravian
Church, Nazareth, Pa.; b. August 10, 1748, Bethlehem, Pa.; d.
November 19, 1815, Nazareth, Pa.

13.   vi.   GOTTLIEB DEMUTH, b. November 18, 1750, Lynn Twp.,
Northampton Co., Pa; d. January 25, 1825, Gnadenhutten, Oh.

14.   vii.   CHRISTOPHER DEMUTH, b. August 22, 1755, Allemaengel, Pa; d.
January 27, 1822, Warwick Twp., Tuscarawas Co., Oh.

    viii.   ROSINA DEMUTH, b. Aft. 1756.

    ix.   CHRISTIAN DEMUTH, b. December 26, 1740, Germantown, Pa.

11. JOHN CHRISTOPHER[3] DEMUTH *(GOTTHARD[2], CHRISTOPH[1])*
was born September 19, 1738 in Germantown, Pa, and died September 7,
1818 in Lancaster, Pa. He married ELIZABETH HARTAFFEL. She was
born October 16, 1746 in Lancaster, Pa.

Children of JOHN DEMUTH and ELIZABETH HARTAFFEL are:

    i.   ANNA MARIA[4] DEMUTH, b. November 9, 1768, Lancaster Co.,
Pa.; m. JOHANNES EBERMAN; b. November 9, 1749.

15.   ii.   JOHANNES DEMUTH, b. December 20, 1771, Lancaster Co., Pa.; d.
March 8, 1822, Lancaster, Pa..

    iii.   FREDERICK DEMUTH, b. June 2, 1773, Lancaster Co., Pa..

    iv.   SOPHIA DEMUTH, b. November 22, 1777, Lancaster Co., Pa.; d.
July 19, 1781, Lancaster Co., Pa..

16.   v.   JACOB DEMUTH, b. August 9, 1778, Lancaster Co., Pa.; d. 1842,
Lancaster, Pa..

17.   vi.   JOSEF DEMUTH, b. October 18, 1781, Lancaster Co., Pa.; d. May
2, 1813, Lancaster Co., Pa..

12. REGINA[3] DEMUTH *(JOHANN CHRISTOPH[2], CHRISTOPH[1])* was
born November 28, 1716, and died March 6, 1779 in Frankebar. She
married (1) PETER DIEHL. She married (2) ? STAHLMANN.

Children of REGINA DEMUTH and PETER DIEHL are:

    i.   MARIA[4] DIEHL, b. 1750; d. 1800.

    ii.   SALOME DIEHL, b. 1754.

Generation No. 4

13. GOTTLIEB[4] DEMUTH *(GOTTLEIB[3], TOBIAS[2], CHRISTOPH[1])* was

153

born November 18, 1750 in Lynn Twp., Northampton Co., Pa, and died January 25, 1825 in Gnadenhutten, Oh. He married ANNA MARIA ALLEMAN April 12, 1773 in Shoeneck, Pa. She was born August 29, 1756 in Warwick, Pa, and died bef. 1820 in Pa.

Children of GOTTLIEB DEMUTH and ANNA ALLEMAN are:

18.   i.   JOSEPH[5] DEMUTH, b. March 22, 1775, Nazareth, Northampton Co., Pa.; d. October 21, 1855, Gnadenhutten, Oh.

19.   ii.   JOHANNES G. DEMUTH, b. November 1, 1777, Northampton Co., Pa.; d. March 13, 1843, Tuscarawas Co., Oh.

    iii.   CHRISTIAN DEMUTH, b. February 14, 1780, Shoeneck, Pa; d. August 29, 1854, Whitehouse, Oh.

    iv.   ANNA MARIA DEMUTH, b. March 19, 1782, Shoeneck, Northampton Co., Pa.

20.   v.   FREDERICK DEMUTH, b. July 18, 1784, Shoeneck, Northampton Co., Pa..

    vi.   RENATUS DEMUTH, b. August 7, 1786, Shoeneck, Northampton Co., Pa.; d. January 3, 1857, Whitehouse, Oh.

    vii.   CATHARINA DEMUTH, b. July 18, 1788, Shoeneck, Northampton Co., Pa.; d. June 29, 1790, Shoeneck, Northampton Co., Pa.

    viii.   WILLIAM GOTTLIEB DEMUTH, b. October 19, 1791, Lancaster Co., Pa.; d. January 28, 1874, Whitehouse, Oh; m. ELIZABETH KIND, abt. 1812; b. May 8, 1797, Lancaster Co., Pa.; d. July 21, 1882, Whitehouse, Oh.

21.   ix.   ABRAHAM JONATHAN DEMUTH, b. February 13, 1794, Shoeneck, Northampton Co., Pa.

    x.   GOTTFRIED BENJAMIN DEMUTH, b. April 2, 1798, Shoeneck, Northampton Co., Pa.; m. SALLY WARD.

14. CHRISTOPHER[4] DEMUTH *(GOTTLIEB[3], TOBIAS[2], CHRISTOPH[1])* was born August 22, 1755 in Allemangel, Pa, and died January 27, 1822 in Warwick Twp., Tuscarawas Co., Oh. He married (1) SUSANNA CATHERINE KLEIN April 8, 1777 in Shoeneck, Pa., daughter of ANDREAS KLEIN and JANE THOMAS. She was born January 2, 1758 in Northampton Co., Pa., and died July 15, 1817 in Warwick, Twp., Tuscarawas Co., Oh. He married (2) ELIZABETH GUNTHER April 16, 1818 in Tuscarawas Co., Ohio.

Children of CHRISTOPHER DEMUTH and SUSANNA KLEIN are:

    i.   JOSEPH[5] DEMUTH, b. January 11, 1778, Northampton Co., Pa..

22.   ii.   JOHN FREDERICK DEMUTH, b. September 11, 1779.

    iii.   SUSANNA CATHERINE DEMUTH, b. May 27, 1781, Northampton Co., Pa.; m. JOHN D. FENNER.

23.   iv.   ANNA ROSINA DEMUTH, b. October 19, 1783, Northampton Co.,

		Pa.; d. September 25, 1860, Tuscarawas Co., Oh.
24.	v.	ANNA MARIA DEMUTH, b. December 29, 1785, Northampton Co., Pa..
25.	vi.	RACHEL ELIZABETH DEMUTH, b. March 15, 1788, Northampton Co., Pa..
26.	vii.	SARAH CATHERINE DEMUTH, b. September 8, 1790, Shoeneck, Plainfield Twp., Northampton Co., Pa; d. September 7, 1850, Gnadenhutten, Oh.
27.	viii.	MARGARETHA DEMUTH, b. March 10, 1793, Northampton Co., Pa..
	ix.	ABIGAIL DEMUTH, b. October 31, 1795, Northampton Co., Pa.; m. JOHN NIEGEMAN.
28.	x.	LYDIA DEMUTH, b. March 22, 1798, Northampton Co., Pa..

15. JOHANNES[4] DEMUTH *(JOHN CHRISTOPHER[3], GOTTHARD[2], CHRISTOPH[1])* was born December 20, 1771 in Lancaster Co., Pa., and died March 8, 1822 in Lancaster, Pa. He married CATHERINE TRISSLER October 20, 1793 in Lititz Moravian Church, Lancaster, Pa. She was born September 30, 1772, and died May 1855.

Children of JOHANNES DEMUTH and CATHERINE TRISSLER are:
- i. CHRISTOPH[5] DEMUTH, b. February 13, 1800; d. March 21, 1831.
- ii. FREDERICK DEMUTH, b. February 23, 1803.
- iii. ELIZABETH DEMUTH, b. April 1, 1805; m. ? HOWELL.
- iv. CATHARINA DEMUTH, b. December 3, 1807; m. HENRY KEPPLE, July 1827, Lancaster, Pa..
- v. SUSANNA DEMUTH, b. January 27, 1812, Lancaster, Pa.; d. May 5, 1812, Lancaster, Pa..
- vi. CHARLES AUGUSTUS DEMUTH, b. January 7, 1810.
- vii. SOPHIA DEMUTH, b. July 7, 1794.

16. JACOB[4] DEMUTH *(JOHN CHRISTOPHER[3], GOTTHARD[2], CHRISTOPH[1])* was born August 9, 1778 in Lancaster Co., Pa., and died 1842 in Lancaster, Pa.. He married (1) ELIZA EBERMAN. She was born January 24, 1783 in Lancaster Co., Pa.. He married (2) CATHERINE MEDFORD December 22, 1807. She was born December 6, 1785.

Child of JACOB DEMUTH and ELIZA EBERMAN is:
- i. EMANUEL EBERMAN[5] DEMUTH, b. December 25, 1804.

Children of JACOB DEMUTH and CATHERINE MEDFORD are:
- ii. EMILIE REGINA LEOPOLDI[5] DEMUTH, b. October 2, 1808.

iii. CARL AUGUSTUS RUDOLPH DEMUTH, b. January 6, 1810.
iv. CAROLINE SUSANNA DEMUTH, b. September 22, 1812.
v. LOUISA ELIZABETH DEMUTH, b. March 5, 1814.
vi. LORENZ ISRAEL DEMUTH, b. September 15, 1815.
vii. SAMUEL CHRISTOPH DEMUTH, b. August 16, 1817.

17. JOSEF[4] DEMUTH *(JOHN CHRISTOPHER[3], GOTTHARD[2], CHRISTOPH[1])* was born October 18, 1781 in Lancaster Co., Pa., and died May 2, 1813 in Lancaster Co., Pa. He married ELIZABETH DANNER May 26, 1805.

Child of JOSEF DEMUTH and ELIZABETH DANNER is:
   i. WILHELM[5] DEMUTH, b. September 16, 1805.

Generation No. 5

18. JOSEPH[5] DEMUTH *(GOTTLIEB[4], GOTTLEIB[3], TOBIAS[2], CHRISTOPH[1])* was born March 22, 1775 in Nazareth, Northampton Co., Pa., and died October 21, 1855 in Gnadenhutten, Oh. He married (1) MARY ANN DOLE September 17, 1797 in York Co., Pa.. She was born November 14, 1755 in Antrim Co., Ireland, and died December 6, 1803 in Lancaster, Pa.. He married (2) CATHERINE SUSANNA SHUMACHER 1806. She was born November 1783, and died January 18, 1840.

Children of JOSEPH DEMUTH and MARY DOLE are:
   i. JOSEPH ALLEN[6] DEMUTH, b. April 30, 1800, Moore Twp., Lancaster Co., Pa.; d. February 20, 1878, Conellsville, Fayette Co., PA; m. JANE RIST.
   ii. ELIZA DEMUTH, m. ? SPIES.
   iii. ANNA MARIA HENRIETTE DEMUTH, b. March 4, 1802, More Twp, Northampton Co., Pa..
   iv. JOHN JOSEPH DEMUTH, b. July 19, 1798, More Twp., Northampton Co., PA.

Children of JOSEPH DEMUTH and CATHERINE SHUMACHER are:
   v. BENJAMIN G.[6] DEMUTH.
   vi. REBECCA DEMUTH, m. ABSOLOM STOCKER, November 30, 1845, Tuscarawas County, Ohio.
   vii. ANNA DEMUTH, b. November 28, 1820; d. November 8, 1850; m. TOBIAS ROMIG, August 29, 1841, Tuscarawas County, Ohio; b. June 1814, Germany; d. August 23, 1865.

156

viii. ELIZA DEMUTH, b. 1827; d. 1914, Iowa City, Iowa; m. SOLOMON HAY.

ix. JOSHUA HIRAM DEMUTH, b. May 2, 1813, Franklin Co., Pennsylvania; d. April 14, 1889, Tuscarawas Co., Ohio; m. ANN ELIZABETH TAYLOR, July 11, 1841; b. December 23, 1817, Tuscarawas Co., Ohio; d. February 22, 1883, Tuscarawas Co., Ohio.

x. DANIEL CHRISTOPHER DEMUTH, b. October 27, 1815; d. October 22, 1864, Tuscarawas Co., Oh; m. MARY MAGDALENA ROTH, December 9, 1838, Tuscarawas County, Ohio; b. April 17, 1821, Nazareth, Northampton Co., Pa.; d. November 30, 1899, Tuscarawas Co., Oh.

19. JOHANNES G.[5] DEMUTH *(GOTTLIEB[4], GOTTLEIB[3], TOBIAS[2], CHRISTOPH[1])* was born November 1, 1777 in Northampton Co., Pa., and died March 13, 1843 in Tuscarawas Co., Oh. He married (1) ELIZABETH RHOADS June 23, 1799 in Pennsylvania. She was born December 13, 1774 in Northampton Co., Pa., and died August 9, 1826 in Gnadenhutten, Oh. He married (2) LYDIA MINSCH April 29, 1827 in Tuscarawas Co., Oh. She was born May 10, 1807 in Gnadenhutten, Oh, and died June 10, 1849.

Children of JOHANNES DEMUTH and ELIZABETH RHOADS are:

i. STEPHEN HARRY[6] DEMUTH, b. June 26, 1800, Plainfield Twp., Northampton Co., Pa.; d. October 6, 1821, Tuscarawas County, Ohio.

ii. DANIEL C. DEMUTH, b. November 30, 1803, Shoeneck, Northampton Co., Pa.; d. July 20, 1848, Tuscarawas Co., Oh; m. (1) MARIA SIMMERS, May 29, 1825, Tuscarawas County, Ohio; d. October 11, 1841, Tuscarawas County, Ohio; m. (2) ELIZABETH WALTON, January 16, 1842, Tuscarawas Co., Oh.

Children of JOHANNES DEMUTH and LYDIA MINSCH are:

iii. THORNTON[6] DEMUTH.

iv. DEBORAH DEMUTH.

v. GEORGE WASHINGTON DEMUTH, m. CASSANDRA BAER, February 21, 1859, Tuscarawas County, Ohio.

vi. AMANDA CATHERINE DEMUTH, b. March 9, 1838, Tuscarawas County, Ohio; d. January 29, 1923, Sedro Wolly, CA.; m. JOSIAH B. ROMIG, May 16, 1858, Tuscarawas County, Ohio.

vii. BENJAMIN FRANKLIN DEMUTH.

viii. REBECCA ANN DEMUTH, b. January 27, 1843; d. March 13, 1843.

20. FREDERICK[5] DEMUTH *(GOTTLIEB[4], GOTTLEIB[3], TOBIAS[2], CHRISTOPH[1])* was born July 18, 1784 in Shoeneck, Northampton Co., Pa.. He married ELIZABETH THOMSON.

Children of FREDERICK DEMUTH and ELIZABETH THOMSON are:
- i. HENRIETTE[6] DEMUTH.
- ii. CECELIA DEMUTH.
- iii. YPSILANTE DEMUTH.
- iv. CHRISTINE REBECCA DEMUTH.
- v. ELVINA DEMUTH.
- vi. SARAH ELIZABETH DEMUTH.
- vii. SUSAN DEMUTH.

21. ABRAHAM JONATHAN[5] DEMUTH *(GOTTLIEB[4], GOTTLEIB[3], TOBIAS[2], CHRISTOPH[1])* was born February 13, 1794 in Shoeneck, Northampton Co., Pa. He married ANNA MARIA SCHNALL October 10, 1819 in Shoeneck, Northampton Co., Pa.

Children of ABRAHAM DEMUTH and ANNA SCHNALL are:
- i. MARIETTA[6] DEMUTH.
- ii. LOUISA DEMUTH.
- iii. HERRIETTE OLIVIE DEMUTH.
- iv. REUBEN THEODORE DEMUTH.
- v. EMA FRANZCIENE DEMUTH.
- vi. GEORGE DEMUTH.

22. JOHN FREDERICK[5] DEMUTH *(CHRISTOPHER[4], GOTTLEIB[3], TOBIAS[2], CHRISTOPH[1])* was born September 11, 1779. He married ELIZABETH ROTH.

Children of JOHN DEMUTH and ELIZABETH ROTH are:
- i. STEPHEN HARRY[6] DEMUTH, b. June 26, 1800, Northampton Co., Pa.; d. October 1821, Gnadenhutten, Oh.
- ii. CHRISTIAN DEMUTH, b. June 14, 1816; d. 1892; m. MARY MCDONALD; b. 1822; d. 1892.
- iii. JOHANNES DEMUTH, b. June 14, 1816.

23. ANNA ROSINA[5] DEMUTH *(CHRISTOPHER[4], GOTTLEIB[3], TOBIAS[2], CHRISTOPH[1])* was born October 19, 1783 in Northampton Co., Pa., and died September 25, 1860 in Tuscarawas Co., Oh. She married

JOSEPH SHAMEL April 2, 1806 in Gnadenhutten, Oh, son of
JOHANNES SHAMEL and ELISABETH HOLDER. He was born
January 17, 1778 in Bethabara, Stokes Co., NC, and died September 29,
1857 in Tuscarawas Co., Oh.

Children of ANNA DEMUTH and JOSEPH SHAMEL are:
     i.   JOHN[6] SHAMEL, b. 1808.
    ii.   JOSEPH SHAMEL, b. 1809.
   iii.   SIBYLLA SHAMEL, b. 1811.
   iv.   ABRAHAM SHAMEL, b. 1813.
    v.   ROSINA CAROL SHAMEL, b. February 12, 1816.
   vi.   ANNA ELIZABETH SHAMEL, b. March 12, 1818.
  vii.   ISAAC SHAMEL, b. 1821.

24. ANNA MARIA[5] DEMUTH *(CHRISTOPHER[4], GOTTLEIB[3],
TOBIAS[2], CHRISTOPH[1])* was born December 29, 1785 in Northampton
Co., Pa.. She married JACOB UHRICH.

Child of ANNA DEMUTH and JACOB UHRICH is:
     i.   BENJAMIN[6] UHRICH, b. March 4, 1816.

25. RACHEL ELIZABETH[5] DEMUTH *(CHRISTOPHER[4], GOTTLEIB[3],
TOBIAS[2], CHRISTOPH[1])* was born March 15, 1788 in Northampton Co.,
Pa. She married RICHARD FERGUSON.

Children of RACHEL DEMUTH and RICHARD FERGUSON are:
     i.   JOHN[6] FERGUSON, b. August 25, 1815.
    ii.   ABIGAIL FERGUSON, b. May 30, 1817.

26. SARAH CATHERINE[5] DEMUTH *(CHRISTOPHER[4], GOTTLEIB[3],
TOBIAS[2], CHRISTOPH[1])* was born September 8, 1790 in Shoeneck,
Plainfield Twp., Northampton Co., Pa, and died September 7, 1850 in
Gnadenhutten, Oh. She married GEORGE SHAMEL December 18, 1810
in Tuscarawas Co., Ohio, son of JOHANNES SHAMEL and ELISABETH
HOLDER. He was born July 21, 1785 in Bethabara, Stokes Co., NC, and
died October 25, 1850 in Gnadenhutten, Tuscarawas Co. Ohio.

Children of SARAH DEMUTH and GEORGE SHAMEL are:
     i.   ABIGAIL[6] SHAMEL, b. October 30, 1811; m. T. INTERLINE, April
         18, 1830.
    ii.   JACOB SHAMEL, b. January 21, 1813; m. CYNTHIA ROBNET,

April 13, 1837, Tuscarawas Co., Ohio.
- iii. WILLIAM SHAMEL, b. October 6, 1814; d. December 16, 1817.
- iv. BENJAMIN SHAMEL, b. March 9, 1817, Warwick Twp., Tuscarawas Co., Oh; m. MARY STANART, March 11, 1841, Tuscarawas Co., Ohio; b. September 25, 1814; d. February 5, 1900.
- v. SARAH CATHERINE SHAMEL, b. April 5, 1819, Tuscarawas Co., Oh; d. October 15, 1850, Orange Twp., Carroll Co., Oh; m. HENRY SMITH, March 19, 1837, Tuscarawas Co. Ohio; b. May 11, 1809, Greene Co., Pa; d. June 21, 1890, Orange Twp., Carroll Co., Oh.
- vi. GOTTLIEB SHAMEL, b. May 26, 1821; m. MARILLA MARTIN, May 23, 1844.
- vii. GEORGE SHAMEL, b. September 28, 1823; m. C. MEYERS, December 5, 1847; b. 1823.
- viii. SUSANA EMILIE SHAMEL, b. March 26, 1826.
- ix. SAMUEL SHAMEL, b. May 9, 1830; d. February 5, 1888; m. SARAH RUTLER; b. August 20, 1829; d. March 25, 1892, Tuscarawas Co., Oh.
- x. ANNA SHAMEL, b. November 16, 1833.

27. MARGARETHA⁵ DEMUTH (CHRISTOPHER⁴, GOTTLEIB³, TOBIAS², CHRISTOPH¹) was born March 10, 1793 in Northampton Co., Pa. She married JOHN FLICKINGER April 7, 1812 in Tuscarawas County, Ohio, son of MICHAEL FLICKINGER and MARY ?. He died 1823.

Children of MARGARETHA DEMUTH and JOHN FLICKINGER are:
- i. CHRISTOPHER⁶ FLICKINGER, b. May 7, 1814.
- ii. LEVI FLICKINGER, b. August 11, 1815, Tuscarawas County, Ohio.
- iii. JOHN FLICKINGER, b. October 9, 1817.
- iv. STEPHEN FLICKINGER, b. May 4, 1823, Tuscarawas County, Ohio; d. January 22, 1869, Union Co., Ohio; m. MARGARET ANNE FIGLEY, August 7, 1845, Tuscarawas County, Ohio; b. December 23, 1825, Tuscarawas County, Ohio; d. July 30, 1886, Union Co., Ohio.

28. LYDIA⁵ DEMUTH (CHRISTOPHER⁴, GOTTLEIB³, TOBIAS², CHRISTOPH¹) was born March 22, 1798 in Northampton Co., Pa., died Bebruary 10, 1822. She married BENJAMIN CASEY.

Child of LYDIA DEMUTH and BENJAMIN CASEY is:
- i. WILLIAM⁶ CASEY, b. July 14, 1817.[152]

---

[152] The information in this Descendants Tree is based on personal research of the author and exchange of information with other Demuth researchers.

BIBLIOGRAPHY

History of the Moravian Church

Clewell, John Henry, *History of Wachovia in North Carolina*, Doubleday Page & Company, 1902.

Dvornik, Francis, *The Slavs in European History and Civilization* by, Rutgers University Press, 1962.

Fries, Adelaide L., *The Moravians in Georgia, 1735-1740*, Edwards & Broughton, Raleigh, 1905.

Hamilton, J. Taylor, and Kenneth G. Hamilton, *History of the Moravian Church, The Renewed Unitas Fratrum, 1727-1957*, 1957.

Hamilton, Kenneth Gardiner, "John Ettwein and the Moravian Church during the Revolutionary Period", *Transactions of the Moravian Historical Society*, Vol. 12, pp. 85-429.

Documentation for some of the information in the Tree is found in the footnotes in Chapters 7 and 8. Much of the information has not been personally documented by the author and is included as an aid or possible lead for persons wishing to do further research on a possible connection to this family. Information in this Tree which is not documented in the footnotes should not be relied upon until it is documented by the researcher.

Hunter, James, *The Quiet People of the Land, A Story of the North Carolina Moravians in Revolutionary Times* 1976

Hutton, J. E., *History of the Moravian Church* Second Edition, Moravian Publication Office, London, 1909.

Langton, Edward, *History of the Moravian Church* George Allen & Unwin, London, 1956

Schattschneider, Allen W., *Through Five Hundred Years, A Popular History of the Moravian Church,* Fourth Edition, The Moravian Church in America, 1996.

Sessler, Jacob John, *Communal Pietism Among the Early American Moravians,* Henry Holt & Company, 1933.

Thorp, Daniel B., *The Moravian Community in Colonial North Carolina,* The University of Tennessee Press, Knoxville.

Weinlick, John R., and Albert H. Frank, *The Moravian Church Through the Ages,* The Moravian Church in America, 1966

The Moravian Missions

Benson, Lillian Rea, "Old Fairfield on the Thames" *Northwest Ohio Quarterly,* Vol. 16, p. 128.

Goehring, Susan, *Schoenbrunn, A Meeting of Cultures,* Ohio Historical Society, 1997

Heckewelder, John, *A Narrative of the Mission of the United Brethren Among the Delaware and Mohegan Indians from its*

Commencement in the year 1740 to the Close of the year 1808, McCarty & Davis, 1820.

Kaufman, Stanley A., and Dr. Lawrence W. Hartzell, *Moravians in Ohio*, German Culture Museum, Walnut Creek, Ohio, 1987.

Olmstead, Earl P., *David Zeisberger, A Life Among the Indians*, Kent State University, 1997.

Olmstead, Earl P., *Blackcoats Among the Delaware, David Zeisberger on the Ohio Frontier*, Kent State University, 1991.

Olmstead, Earl P., "A Day of Shame, the Gnadenhutten Story", *Timeline*, the Ohio Historical Society, August/September 1991, Vol. 8, No. 4 pp. 21-33.

Wallace, Paul A., *Thirty Thousand Miles with John Heckewelder*, Pittsburgh: University of Pittsburgh Press, 1958.

The Ohio Frontier and The Indian Wars

Booth Jr., Russell H., *The Tuscarawas Valley in Indian Days, 1750-1797*, Gomber House Press, Cambridge, Ohio, 1994.

Butterfield, C.W., *The Expedition Against Sandusky under Col. William Crawford in 1782*, Robert Clarke & Company, 1873.

Butterfield, C.W., *Washington-Irvine Correspondence*, D. Atwood, Madison, Wisconsin, 1882.

Eckert, Allan W., *That Dark and Bloody River*, Bantam Books, 1995

Hassler, Edgar W., *Old Westmoreland, A History of Western Pennsylvania During the Revolution,* 1900, reprint by Heritage Books, 1998

Hurt, R. Douglas, *The Ohio Frontier, Crucible of the Old Northwest 1720-1830,* Indiana University Press, 1996.

Knepper, George W., *Ohio and Its People,* Kent State University Press, 1989

Koontz, Louis K., *The Virginia Frontier, 1754-1763,* John Hopkins Press, 1925, reprint by Heritage Books, 1992.

Nelson, Larry L., *A Man of Distinction Among Them, Alexander McKee and British Indian Affairs Along the Ohio Country Frontier 1754-1799,* Kent State University Press, 1999

Nelson, Larry L., *Men of Patriotism Courage & Enterprise, Fort Meigs in the War of 1812,* Heritage Books, 1997

Sugden, John, *Tecumseh, A Life,* Henry Holt and Company, 1997

Sugden, John, *Blue Jacket, Warrior of the Shawnees* University of Nebraska Press, 2000

Weslager, C.A., *The Delaware Indians, A History,* Rutgers University Press, New Brunswick, N.J. 1972

Withers, Alexander S., *Chronicles of Border Warfare* 1831, reprint by Heritage Books, 1993

The Demuth Family

Battershell, C.F., *The Demuth Family and the Moravian Church,* Seibert Printing Co., Dover, Ohio, 1931.

Genson, Chloe, *William Gottleib Demuth, His Ancestors and Descendants,* 1994.

Kluge, Rev. Edward T., "Moravian Graveyards at Nazareth, Pa. 1744-1904", *Transactions of the Moravian Historical Society* Vol. 7, pp. 90-91, 95.

Milligan, Fred J., *Christoph Demuth and Susanna Catherine (Klein) Demuth, Moravian Pioneers at Gnadenhutten, Tuscarawas County, Ohio,* Millstone Publications, 1997.

Niesser, George, "A List of the Bohemian and Moravian Emigrants to Saxony", *Transactions of the Moravian Historical Society,* Vol. 9, pp. 41-93.

Rechcigl, Jr., Miloslav, "The Demuth Genealogy Revisited: A Moravian Brethren Family from Czechoslovakia*", Journal of the Lancaster County Historical Society,* Vol. 92, No.2 pp. 55-68.

Rechcigl, Jr., Miloslav , "Another Visit to Moravian Demuths" *News and History of the Demuth Families* published by Patrick Demuth, Worthington, MN No. 21, p. 206.

Monument to Tuscarawas County Soldiers of the Revolutionary War

ABOUT THE AUTHOR

The author is an attorney who has served as general counsel of the Ohio Historical Society for over 25 years. He learned a love for Ohio history from his father who served as a member of the board of trustees, president and general counsel of the Society. He believes that history is important not only for what it says about the past, but more importantly for what it says about the present and the future. The author and his wife are descended from Ohio pioneer families. Ohio will be celebrating its bicentennial in 2003. He researched the Demuth family as part of a family bicentennial project to research the lives of each of their pioneer ancestors. His wife and children are descendants of the Demuths. Upon discovering that the President is also a descendant of this family, he thought others might enjoy reading about the fascinating story of the Moravians and the Demuth family's role in that story. The author believes that every family's history is important and interesting if sufficient time is taken to understand how each life related to what was going on around it. He also believes that Americans will gain from a study of their family's history a greater sense of what is important in life and what is important for America as a nation.

INDEX

171

172

173